1995-1-PB

004
C28

S0-CBT-271

...internet.

Niles Community Library
620 E. Main Street
Niles, Michigan 49120

NOV 1 9 1996

DEMCO

NILES COMMUNITY LIBRARY

3 3004 00124 3040

CHILDPROOF INTERNET:

A Parent's Guide to Safe and Secure Online Access

Matt Carlson

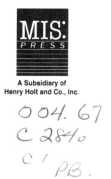

MIS: PRESS

A Subsidiary of
Henry Holt and Co., Inc.

004. 67
C 2840
C 1
PB.

A Subsidiary of
Henry Holt and Co., Inc.

Copyright © 1996, by MIS:Press.
a subsidiary of Henry Holt and Company, Inc.
115 West 18th Street
New York, NY 10011
http://www.mispress.com

All rights reserved. Reproduction or use of editorial or pictorial content in any manner is prohibited without express permission. No patent liability is assumed with respect to the use of the information contained herein. While every precaution has been taken in the preparation of this book, the publisher assumes no responsibility for errors or omissions. Neither is any liability assumed for damages resulting from the use of the information contained herein.

Throughout this book, trademarked names are used. Rather than put a trademark symbol after every occurrence of a trademarked name, we used the names in an editorial fashion only, and to the benefit of the trademark owner, with no intention of infringement of the trademark. Where such designations appear in this book, they have been printed with initial caps.

First Edition—1996

Printed in the United States of America.

Library of Congress Cataloging-in-Publication Data

ISBN 1-55828-499-0

10 9 8 7 6 5 4 3 2 1

MIS:Press books are available at special discounts for bulk purchases for sales promotions, premiums, and fundraising. Special editions or book excerpts can also be created to specification.

For details contact: Special Sales Director
                          MIS:Press
                          a subsidiary of Henry Holt and Company, Inc.
                          115 West 18th Street
                          New York, New York 10011

Associate Publisher: *Paul Farrell*

Executive Editor: *Cary Sullivan*   **Production Editor:** *Stephanie Doyle*
Editor: *Andrew Neusner*   **Technical Editor:** *John Munnell*
Copy Edit Manager: *Shari Chappell*   **Copy Editor:** *Jack Donner*

DEDICATION

To my children…

"The future has several names.
For the weak, it is the impossible.
For the fainthearted, it is the unknown.
For the thoughtful and valiant, it is ideal"

—*Victor Hugo*

ACKNOWLEDGMENTS

I want to thank all of those who have encouraged me to write this book not because I am such a great writer but because they had the vision and foresight to see the need for the information and encouraged me to write about something I am passionate about...helping others.

To my mentor and friend Dennis Kimbro whose Nike-like "Just Do It" attitude made the leap from quiet contentment to action possible. His instructions to write everyday, everyday, everyday are emblazoned on my mind forever. To David Melton and Ron Greer without whose support I couldn't and wouldn't have continued the quest. To John Munnell whose technical guidance has kept this book in the realm of fact rather than science fiction and to the editors—Paul Farrell, Andy Neusner and Stephanie Doyle—who were willing to take on a first time author and guide me patiently & painstakingly through the process of getting to print. To all of you I owe a deep debt of gratitude and thanks.

It would be impossible to thank all those who contributed to the research because they are the many hundreds who have attended the Safe Surfing Seminars we have conducted throughout the United States during the past 18 month. With each presentation and parent, the depth and breadth of my understanding of the challenges the on-line world poses for today's families grew.

To my kids who keep me from becoming cynical and remind me in their daily actions that a simpler, more innocent world still exists—Thank you.

And finally to my wife, who has read over countless versions and drafts, proofread final copy and loved me through it all—Thank you and I love you....

Contents

Foreword

A Call to Action

Regardless of what new technology comes along or how it is used, our roles as parents do not change; what changes is how we do them. This is especially true today. We protect our children from the harms of drugs, gangs, and pornography. To do so, we lock our cars and doors at night to keep out the dangers that threaten us. Now, parents are confronted with the Internet, a technology that can bring those very problems within the walls of our home, perhaps without our knowledge. As parents we educate, guide, instill values, and give purpose to our children's lives. Technology that can assist and enhance those roles should be welcomed. But when the same technology threatens the safety and well-being of our family, we must act. That is what this book is about—*action*!

As a parent of two children and an educator at heart (if not always by profession), I was concerned when I began to hear of and then see the type of information that is available on the Internet. My original concern was for kids, but as I talked with parents and educators I was concerned for them as well. I became concerned for the parents who seem resigned to the fact that one day they would have to follow the road of technology and use the Internet, doing so without concern, or perhaps the willingness, to find out where it is taking them. Technology is not a destination, it is a tool. It is a means to an end, to a brighter future, a more informed world, a more educated and accepting place. Yes, but at what cost? As parents we cannot follow blindly, abdicating our responsibilities under the guise of "I don't know how." This book gives you the opportunity to learn *how*, the question is: will you?

1

This book is for parents whose kids use (or will use) technology, not for computer wizards who happen to have kids. Quite honestly I could not have written the latter. In writing the book, I have made the assumption that you are familiar with your computer, whether it runs Windows or DOS or is a Macintosh. You should be familiar with using a mouse and launching applications from your desktop.

Throughout the book I have also inserted lessons I have learned from our seminars and my work with parents, educators, and kids. It would have been easy to bury these stories deep in the text but I have set them off because they often represent the very heart of the matter at hand. I hope you enjoy my musings.

The ultimate solution to the issues raised by this book is no different from the ones for sex or alcohol or drugs. Parents must be ready, willing, and able to step up to the role of parenting. Willing to put aside our fears, confront our ignorance, and get a hold of the issues so we can deal with them logically, sanely, and safely. Nothing I put between the covers of this book will make a parent ready or willing, but when they are, the chapters of this book will certainly make them able.

When asked if I think I can really make a difference in the face of so great a challenge as technology and the Internet, I often share the story of the man on the beach who walked down the beach each morning at dawn picking up the starfishes abandoned by the tide and putting each one back into the ocean. When asked if he really thought he could make a difference in so great a challenge he replied, "Maybe not but I made a difference to that one" as he gingerly placed another starfish back among the waves. This book is about what *you* can do. Not on a national level or with associations or groups but rather at the fundamental building block of our society—your home. It is time that we as parents learn about technology and the Internet so that we can assist and protect our children. God bless and good reading.

Matt Carlson

High Tech Parenting: A Whole New World

Cyberspace … Chat rooms … Hard drive … RAM … Modem … Yahoo
…Information super highway … World Wide Web … Internet …
America Online … Home page … e-mail … Webcrawler …

These words and phrases that were nonexistent just a few years ago are now part of nearly everyone's vocabulary—even if people don't really understand what the words mean. For many of you, these words strike fear in your hearts and make you break out in a cold sweat. You are not alone. For many parents, computers are still a magical box. Many of us have used them in the office and know our way around standard spreadsheet and word processing programs. But, when it comes to whizzing around the world, jumping from Web page to Web page, participating in multifaceted chat sessions or even exchanging information with people we do not know and will probably never meet (at least in person), we are reluctant and scared. On the other hand, our kids are as comfortable with these activities as going to the mall.

> The issue is one of innovation and changing paradigms and our willingness to accept that change. To put it in perspective, step back 20 years with me. Imaging how your parents felt about calculators, LCD watches, and cassette and 8-track tapes. But if I had stepped up just as you were plugging the new 8-track player into your car and told you that in ten years you would be getting your music from four-inch silver disks, that we would all have phones in our cars, and that our mail would be sent to our homes via the phone and would print out on something called a fax machine, what would you have thought?

Is it any wonder then, that a walk through a local high school leaves us feeling that technology has left us behind? Libraries have been replaced by media centers run by media specialists are not librarians. A broadcast studio and closed circuit television long ago replaced the principal reading morning announcements on the loud speaker. "Keyboarding" sounds more like something you should do at the beach than in typing classes. Labs of thirty, forty, fifty computers that are linked to each other and the instructor's computer are commonplace for teaching word processing, desktop publishing, spreadsheet applications, and computer programming—yes, programming—in the middle and high schools.

Computers in the classroom serve a variety of purposes, from teaching phonics and reading skills to unlocking the wonders of calculus to analyzing the temperature and viscosity of a liquid in a chemistry class. Is it any wonder then that our children are so excited about what they can do with technology and ask for—in fact demand—access to that same technology at home? Because you are uncomfortqable with the new technology, your natural reaction will be to resist change. But sooner or later you realize there is no stopping the change, so you adapt and conform. Because, after all, is it fair to deny your children access to that technology when doing so is really the equivalent of locking the door to the library in today's electronic society?

During a recent visit to a high school computer club, I was introduced to Michael, a bright and outgoing sophomore. It turned out that Michael had started the computer club at the school two years ago when he was getting ready to enter the ninth grade and was concerned about the lack of computer use at the high school he would be attending the next year! As I talked with Michael, I learned that he had started programming in Basic and Pascal when he was nine. Now he was interested in C++ and object-oriented programming. Michael told me that he had designed home pages for several major corporations and worked on a contract basis for a local service provider helping businesses get on the Internet. Imagine a 15-year-old whose computer skills would meet and exceed more than 50% of a given Sunday's data processing classifieds— Experienced programmer, minimum five years experience, familiarity with most current languages, client/server experience desirable, IBM and Mac experience a must—these are the people who are just entering high school!

I know many of you are thinking, "my kids aren't into computers," and you are probably right. *But whatever they are into is on the computer, and therein lies the difference.* To our kids, computers are just a tool … a means to an end. Technology is another way of expanding their horizons, whether they are interested in the NBA, the FDA, the NFL, or cooking, racing machines, or sewing machines.

In the Beginning

Because it seemed that parents were operating under a technological disadvantage, a year ago my colleagues and I at Safety Net Services began talking to kids, parents, educators, family counselors, and "the experts" about technology. We discussed a range of topics from television and computers to the Internet and cyberspace. We talked about the changing role of computers, and finally we talked about where technology is headed and how it will affect our lives. Not surprisingly, my colleagues and I got lots of different answers, but one thing became particularly clear—the views of parents, and to some extent of educators, were radically different from those of the kids and technology experts. It is clear that today there exists a technology gap between parents and their kids.

This technology gap, created by children's eagerness (or at least willingness) to embrace technology and their parent's fear and ignorance of that same technology, was the genesis for our company. Based on our research, we developed educational programs for parents and educators that would teach them about:

○ Computers and the Internet;

○ How technology is being used today in business, in the classroom, and at home;

○ The dark side of technology, and finally;

○ Options for managing technology to create a bridge rather than a wedge between parents and their children.

Within weeks we were inundated with requests for information regarding our programs. Requests came from school boards, educators, parent teacher organizations, religious organizations, and most of all from parents. Since last summer our company has conducted hundreds of seminars, spoken at conferences, and addressed radio and television audiences with one goal in mind: to close the technology gap between parents and their children. As a parent, if you are not ready to go online, don't feel bad. Most parents who attend our seminar initially have no desire to get online. Rather, they attend in order to understand what their children are doing and why, to learn why they should invest in technology for their children, and generally to quiet their fears about their children gaining access to inappropriate material. However, several weeks later, we get calls from parents asking when our next hands-on seminar is or inquiring what to do next.

High-Tech Parenting

Peter Drucker, acknowledged by many as the management guru of the last 25 years, asserts in his book, *Post Capitalist Society*, that "every few hundred years in Western history there occurs a sharp transformation. Within a few short decades, society rearranges itself, its world view, its basic values, its social and political structure, its arts and its key institutions. Fifty years later, there is a new world. And the people born then cannot ever imagine the world in which their own parents were born."[1] It was true for Columbus, Gutenberg, Adam Smith, Charles Lindbergh, and Neil Armstrong. Few would dispute that we are once again at the leading edge of such a transformation. A transformation to an age of information and convenience never before imagined. I am often asked about what will happen in the next five to ten years and the only thing I can state with certainty is that if I were to make a prediction it would most certainly be wrong. This transformation is happening so fast that technology being developed today runs the risk of being obsolete before it is ever released to the market.

> Though there are many examples of technology that became obsolete during development, a recent and painful example for many electronics companies is that of High Definition Television (HDTV). This much-celebrated technology that was heralded as the next generation of television took so long in development that superior technologies were developed, released, and adopted before HDTV could be introduced—all in the span of two to three years.

Most experts agree that it will be several decades before we see the complete depth and breadth of the transformation to an information age of which most of you reading this book will only feel the side effects. Perhaps you have already begun to feel some of those side effects. Only four or five pages back you were ready to label me a lunatic, and yet CDs are a reality, 8-track tapes and the vinyl record industry are gone. These changes are all possible because of a shift in your old paradigms—you had to go to the teller to get money, Joe came out to pump your gas, and you had to go to the store to purchase your goods. Today you are using ATMs, paying for gas at the pump, and shopping from home via phone, modem, and fax. These conveniences are only the beginning of what this new age will bring. However, our children's lives and careers will be forever changed by this transformation. In fact, many of our children will play pivotal roles in shaping its future. One last thing to remember about innovation and changing paradigms: As Joel Barker states in his well-known video, *The Business of Paradigms*... "when paradigms shift, everything goes back to zero, none of the old rules apply."[2] So the next time you are faced with technology that leaves you feeling threatened, scared, or lost just remember, none of the old rules apply.

How All This Affects Today's Parents

There are many facets to the evolution of an information age, but three majors events have shaped the issues discussed in this book:

- ○ Steady increase in the use of computers, with a rising trend toward usage in the home.

- ○ Dramatic increase in the use of the Internet (and commercial online services).

- ○ Development of a technology gap between parents and children as a result of parents' slow assimilation of technology.

As technology becomes faster, cheaper, and more user friendly, more adults will accept technology and begin using it in unprecedented ways. But before this happens, several generations of parents will be faced with the uncomfortable role of parenting in a high-tech world. To more thoroughly understand the issues and lay the ground work for bridging the technology gap, let's look at each of the driving events in detail.

The Increased Use of Personal Computers

A number of circumstances have put us at the edge of the information age, but unquestionably the most significant has been the advent of the personal computer. Computers have become such an integral part of our lives that it is easy to forget that the first personal computer was introduced in 1980. In fact, the very first computer in the world was built in the late 1940s. As recently as the mid-1970s computers less powerful than the one used to write this book occupied whole rooms and cost millions of dollars. Only now are the first generation of children who have used computers since childhood graduating from college.

COMPUTERS ARE GETTING EASIER TO USE

The first phenomenon driving the increased use of computers is their improved ease of use. The very first personal computers were slow and bulky. Commands consisted of strings of text, and you constantly had to refer to the user manual. Data could only be stored on magnetic disks. (How many of you remember the 11-inch floppy disks of that era?) The cost of these beasts was astronomical, while computing power and applications outside of word processing were severely limited. Programming as it were was a cumbersome, nonintuitive process that used languages such as Basic or COBOL. Those who mastered these computer languages achieved almost mystical status.

Those computers are a far cry from the ultra-fast computers of today. Today's desktop computers can store hundreds of thousands of pages of text, keep our schedules, check our mail, balance our checkbooks, buy the groceries, make sales presentations to clients thousands of miles away, and yet they take up less space than a small television.

All this may be meaningless to you, but what it demonstrates is that computers have finally reached the point where they are fast enough, easy enough, and cheap enough that almost anyone can own one. Many who considered the computer a luxury item just a few years ago are bringing them into their homes to explore this strange new world. While that may sound like science fiction to some, for the last two years computers have outsold televisions in the United States by significant margins. Why this swing in the adaptation of technology?

The argument of whether Apple or IBM is better will rage on well beyond the life of this book. No one will dispute however, that Apple's introduction of the Macintosh computer with it's "happy Mac" icon, point-and-click mouse, and intuitive user interface was responsible for introducing the computer to the school environment and opening the door to the explosion of computer use. Few other computer inventions have had as much to do with the migration of the computer from office to school to home than the mouse and the point-and-click world in which it operates. So successful was Apple's interface at winning new users that within a few years Microsoft Corporation replicated Apple's interface with the release of Windows. Today, the computer is so simple that children as young as three or as old as ninety can easily turn the computer on and find their way to interactive stories, games, or educational programs without reading manuals or receiving outside help.

THE ROLE OF THE COMPUTER IS CHANGING

In addition to ease of use, the changing role of the computer is driving the dramatic increase in computer usage. FIND/SVP and Grunwald Associates conducted a survey in 1995 and determined that the main reason for a family buying a PC has changed from parents' working at home to the kids' educational needs. Nearly three-quarters of the households studied reported that their television viewing declined dramatically when a multimedia computer was introduced into the home. As educators continue to warm up to computers and introduce new uses, children's use of CD-ROM and online encyclopedias, word processors, desktop publishing, and online services will increase well beyond current levels. In our work with educators, my company has assisted with the development of dynamic lesson plans that include significant use of online resources outside the classroom for research and the development of background materials.

> Educators across the nation continue to embrace the new technologies that are available to them. During our recent work with a Georgia public school system, we learned of requirements by many instructors that their students use no less that three types of resources when completing term papers, only one of which could be the printed word. In addition to computers for research, we found computers employed in science classrooms as test equipment, in foreign language labs for interactive work with students in foreign countries and virtual field trips to the countries whose language they are studying, in math labs to model complex mathematical equations, and finally in the administrative offices for more traditional office applications.

Another change in the role of the computer is who is using it. According to the FIND/SVP study, mom is now as likely to use the computer as dad, and usage between young girls and boys is evenly split. More and more computers are finding their way out of the word processing and spread-sheet environment of the office and into the communication, education, exploration, information, and "life management" roles of the home. So prevalent is the use of computers that by the end of 1996, it is projected that more than one in three homes in the United States will have a home PC and by the year 2000 that number will be greater than 40 percent. That is almost one in two homes. So, is that you or your neighbor? You say you are not sure? That's OK, neither was I.

COMPUTERS ARE GETTING CHEAPER

Finally, as the demand for PCs has grown, so has the supply and competition among manufacturers, and subsequently prices have dropped. Only five years ago, a cutting-edge computer would have cost $5000 or more (that machine, a 286 clone, sits in my office as a testimony to a bygone era). Today, a brand new, "hot rod" PC with a very fast Pentium processor and all the bells and whistles only costs about $1500 to $2000, including modem, speakers, CD-ROM and tons of pre-loaded software, and operating system.

So narrow are the profit margins in PCs today that only the large computer superstores remain open where many small retail shops once stood. Two-thousand dollars is still a significant expenditure to most American families, but not so much that it has prevented them from buying more computers than televisions for the last two years! In fact, more computers were purchased as Christmas gifts in 1995 than ever before.

One last development worth mentioning is the persistent talk in the industry of an "Internet only" computer. This stripped-down version of a desktop computer would only allow Internet access and would cost between $300 and $500. Additionally, several electronics manufacturers have announced plans to offer devices that resemble cable TV converter boxes that will allow Internet access from the cable TV company through the television. The estimated price of these boxes is also $300 to $500. One can only speculate what effect these developments will have on the personal computer industry. But one thing is clear: computers are here to stay, they are being used at record rates by more and more homes, and in the opinion of this author "we ain't seen nothin' yet!"

The Evolving Role of the Internet

The Internet. A network of networks interconnecting more than 250,000 networks, millions of host sites, and approximately 40–50 million users around the world. Computers interconnected to share data, have conversations, exchange ideas, and, yes, sell things, shrink the world down until it fits into a box no bigger that the television. Conservative estimates put more than 100 million users on the Internet by the year 2000.

The Internet started out as a tool to increase communication between users. Recent studies however, show that the Internet is more often being used as a source for information and a new form of entertainment. Many people are using the Internet in lieu of more traditional forms of entertainment like movies, television, outdoor recreation, or even reading. The reason? Many people joining the Internet today are not techno-wizards but rather people looking to expand their world beyond what time and money would otherwise allow. Leading the charge in this global expansion of knowledge are our kids.

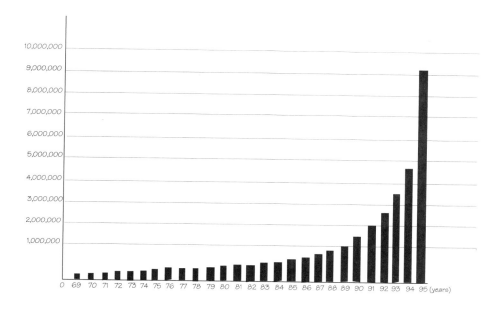

Figure 1.1 Internet hosts.

On a recent afternoon, my daughter and I went on a safari—a cyber-safari that is. For an hour we roamed the deserts of Africa without ever leaving the comfort of my home office. Earlier that day I had seen a reference to a site on the World Wide Web about the African desert. When my daughter came home I put the monitor, keyboard, and mouse on the floor, and we were off. The screen came to life with sights and sounds and videos of life on the Serenghetti. When we saw animals that were unfamiliar we went to an online encyclopedia and looked them up. We joined chat groups about Africa, and in less than a minute had responses from Europe and Africa about what a real safari experience is like. My daughter's eyes weren't the only ones wide with excitement. The only downside of our "trip" is that one of the questions that is now asked on a weekly basis is "Papa when are we going to Africa?"

You don't have to listen to Vice President Al Gore saying that it is both his vision and that of the Clinton administration to make the Internet available to virtually every school in the United States very often before you begin to believe it. Dozens of programs have been initiated to make hardware, access, and training available to educators and community officials. Many of our politicians are looking for ways to improve education and see the Internet as a significant tool to raise the quality of education especially in rural areas where funding constraints often hamper improvement programs. The number of grants available from federal and state sources for developing new technologies, new uses in and out of the classroom, and educator development and training is proof positive of the sincerity behind the words.

Over the past several years, schools have seen a dramatic increase in the use of the Internet. Fueled by corporate donations, private donations, and federal and state grants, numerous schools have created a presence on the Internet.

President Clinton Kicks Off NetDay96

March 3, 1996—President Bill Clinton and Vice President Al Gore kicked off NetDay96, a cooperative effort of corporations, local businesses, school districts, parents, and students to bring the Internet to the classroom in Concord, California. Clinton labeled the effort "an inspiration to the nation. In a way, NetDay is a modern version of an old-fashioned barn-raising... Government is not doing this alone, nor is business nor can schools do it alone. All of us are joining together," said Clinton. "What you are doing today is America at its very best and is guaranteeing America's future. We are putting the future at the fingertips of your children and we are doing it together in the best American tradition. We must not send our children into the twenty-first century unprepared for the world they will inhabit and the jobs they will have to fill." Clinton's call for a

$2 billion fund to be used to encourage matching donations from the private sector to bring computer technology to classrooms across the nation comes at a time when public opinion polls show the majority of Americans feel uneasy about their futures and those of their children, in part because of the rapid changes brought about by technology.

For many schools today, the Internet is little more than a place to post information about the school: its address and phone number, some limited student data, and activities information. However, as Internet access spreads to more than a few computers in any given school, it will take on a much more dynamic role. Some of the more advanced schools already use the Internet for submitting homework, scheduling, class registration, notes to parents, grades, email between students and faculty, and research both inside and outside the classroom, and some have plans for live video conferencing and long-distance learning centers.

So what is next? Where is the Internet headed? Today, there is an incredible amount of information on the Internet—much of it free. Within the next few years, even more information will be available. Commercial use of the Internet is expected to increase tenfold. Today, universities, government agencies, businesses, educators, and students all use the Internet. Many future applications will make the Internet "transparent" to people who are using it. The Internet and your computer will be integrated to perform vital functions without you having to be involved in the nuts-and-bolts computer end of it. How its role will evolve is anybody's guess, but the fact that it will evolve and continue to grow is undisputed.

The Technology Gap: Creek or Chasm?

With all the talk of computers and the Internet, technology replacing jobs, high tech in our schools and homes, it is no surprise most parents my company has spoken with feel left behind by the information age. Of the thousands of parents we visit, fewer than 1 percent say that they have a grasp of today's technology and the role it plays in their children's lives. The result is a technology gap. To understand the magnitude of this gap, most of us need only think back to our own youth when changes in social attitudes and the role of government during the 1960s and 1970s created the generation gap. Now multiply that gap by 10, 50, 100 times and you can begin to understand the challenge the "technology gap" will present. Of greater concern is the fact that very few parents have any idea about how to deal with that gap.

There are two fundamental reasons for this gap—lack of knowledge and fear. Computers were thrust upon many of us in our workplace as a way to increase productivity and efficiency. The machine that started out as merely a replacement for the typewriter soon created data that could be analyzed to point out our every weakness and mistake. Soon computers seemed to dictate every facet of our daily lives. Because most of us didn't or couldn't see the role technology would play in the future, we chose to let others be the computer people. Like so many other times through history, we shot arrows at the pioneers, gave them funny names, and ridiculed and mocked them. When we finally woke up and realized how profound the effects of technology would be, we felt left behind. Today, the computer remains a "magic box" to many, capable of great mystical feats. The result is a fear of the unknown.

If you are one of the people I just described, I want to assure you that it is never too late to begin using computers. In fact, computers today are in many cases easier to operate than your VCR. Many people are afraid to touch the mouse or press on the keyboard for fear they will break something. And for those of you whose VCR is still flashing 12:00, fear not. Computers are not as fragile as the techno-wizards lead us to believe, and if the thing really does run away with you and get completely out of control just remember, you know where the plug is.

The final step for most parents, and seemingly more so for men than women, is the move from unconscious incompetence to conscious incompetence, which is followed quickly by a general fear of public ridicule if they were to they should we admit we are ignorant about computers and what they can do?

Most of our seminar participants are women. This has always amused me. When I inquire why their husbands are not in attendance, invariably the response is that he sent me to get the information and I'm to tell him. The husband was afraid that by coming he might expose his ignorance.

The fear of the unknown and the fear of exposure are further compounded by the fear all parents face when a child slips from under their protective wing. This happens early in the area of technology because, unlike many things where experience has given us knowledge, we have no experience base from which to guide our children's actions. The reaction from many parents faced with this issue is, "If we don't understand it we can't control it and if we can't control it then it is something to be feared." Unfortunately, more often than not, parents' reaction to these fears is to deny their children access to technology and to make futile attempts at forcing technological abstinence on their children because of their own unwillingness to gather the requisite knowledge and confront the issue head on.

Other Defining Events

Several other issues serve to compound the three issues we have discussed so far. Although none of these has anywhere near the impact of the major issues, they simply throw gasoline on a smoldering fire.

LACK OF RESOURCES AVAILABLE TO PARENTS

When it comes to technology education, and more specifically the Internet, parents often find that the resources necessary to help them gather the required background are woefully inadequate. Educators have school district specialists and technical consultants to assist them. Students rely on other students and educators to expand their knowledge base. Parents, turning to the usual sources of information, will all too often find a void of information. Typical educational resources for parents include colleagues, peers, clergy, and friends. In most cases, these individuals have no more knowledge than the parent. Periodicals and newspapers often identify parents' fears in broad-brush articles (as if they needed reminding) but offer little in the way of advice to resolve the issues. A walk down the parenting aisle of the local bookstore will leave you empty handed. Computer books often make the assumption that the reader knows far more than he actually does. Further, the information does not help to identify issues and concerns of parents but rather those of the common user. Often, the best computer education resources available to parents are hands-on courses offered by local colleges and universities. These institutions often have the facilities and instructors with sufficient background to address questions that range from the most fundamental to the most advanced.

AVAILABILITY OF INAPPROPRIATE INFORMATION

The biggest concern we hear voiced by parents about the use of technology and the Internet is the proliferation of material inappropriate for children and the seeming inability of technology to restrict access to this material. While part of this argument is fact and part hype, material inappropriate for children does exist and should be carefully managed. White supremacist groups use the Internet to share propaganda and conduct hate speech campaigns against minority groups. New Jersey police recently blamed an outbreak of bombings on information downloaded from the Internet by teenagers. Unscrupulous brokers and scam artists use online services to lure people into risky or fraudulent investments. Pedophiles share child pornography online and use chat groups to win children's confidences and lure them to clandestine meetings. It is this very topic that prompted me to write this book. There *are* actions parents can take to make cyberspace safe. So what's the fuss all about? We will discuss this matter in depth in the next chapter.

FOOTNOTES

[1]*Post Capitalist Society*, Peter F. Drucker, Harper Business, 1993, pp. 103

[2]*The Business of Paradigms* (video cassette), Joel A. Barker, Charterhouse Learning Corporation, 1989

Involved Parents:
The Only Real Solution

Now that we have laid the ground work, let's discuss what this book is all about: creating a safe and sane place for our kids to play with the technology that will equip them for the twenty-first century.

Few parents are unaware that bomb recipes, hate speech, and pornographic materials are available on the Internet. While these materials comprise a very small percentage of the information available on the Internet (estimates range from half a percent to 5 percent), parents' concerns about their kids' exposure to such material are legitimate, and the natural reaction of any parent to a threat to their children is to protect them. For most parents, the only protection from technology they know is abstinence—pull the plug. It is interesting however, that the same parents who agree that trying to teach teens abstinence from sex is about as productive as teaching a pig to sing are the parents who use abstinence as a way to protect their children from the ills of technology.

NILES COMMUNITY LIBRARY
NILES, MICHIGAN 49120

Why are such materials available? Can't someone do something about it? These are the two most common questions we hear from parents around the country. In Chapter 6, we will address the options available for confronting this issue, but before we do, let's explore what types of material you should be aware of and why the only real option for parents is to become involved in what their kids are doing online and to monitor their kids' activities either personally or electronically.

Why Inappropriate Materials are Available

It is important to remember that there is nothing on the Internet that isn't available in other places. Pornography, hate speech, and sexually explicit material and conversations are just as available through magazines, catalogs, 1-800 and 1-900 phone numbers, and many other sources as on the Internet. Some of these materials are even available in local libraries. Just like in real life, prostitution, pornography, bigotry, and crimes of all types exist to varying degrees, so it is with the Internet. The fact is that as long as pornography and other undesirable materials are present in society at large they will be present on the Internet. Most people would like these things to go away in real life as well, but the justice system has yet to do away with all crime and the courts have repeatedly upheld the First Amendment rights of individuals to create and distribute tasteless material. Why should we expect it to be any different online?

The reason this material exists online in the first place is simple—the Internet isn't something you can touch or feel, someone you can try for crimes and send to jail. It is just people.

The Internet is an enigma. It is not a place or a company. You can't write to it and it has no headquarters and no president. The Internet is a nongeographically based communication medium that is truly international in scope. Essentially, it brings together a cross section of the many cultures that span the globe to create its own 30-million-member society.

Although numerous organizations have been instrumental in establishing the Internet, creating standards, and even funding it, no one owns the Internet. Consequently, no single entity is responsible or can be held accountable for the information available on the Internet. This single fact makes controlling the material on the Internet almost impossible.

The issue is compounded by the international aspect of the Internet. Even though the Internet began in the United States, it does not give Americans the right to impose our standards of right and wrong on the world any more than creation of the United Nations would give us similar rights. The Internet is an international tool whose users are subject only to their own nation's sovereignty. Our ideas regarding right and wrong and the laws we have to enforce those beliefs do not—and should not—extend to the rest of the world. This creates a situation, however, that allows information that would normally be outside the bounds of common decency within our community, state, or country to infiltrate our libraries, our schools, and finally our homes.

Examples of Inappropriate Material

Fueling the fears of many parents are the concerns raised about inappropriate material on the Internet. However, all too often parents choose to look the other way or assume their kids "wouldn't do those things." As a result, parents have only a vague idea that an issue exists but no concept of the magnitude of the problem. The following summary should make you aware of the various types of material available online. It should not take the place of your dedicating some time online to fully understand the issue.

> Despite the publicity and hype that the availability of inappropriate material on the Internet has received in the press, the most frequent response my company hears from parents is, "I had no idea how bad some of the material is and how easy it is to get to." All too often, parents find out too late that it is very difficult to control something they don't understand.

PORNOGRAPHIC AND SEXUALLY EXPLICIT MATERIAL

- ○ Traditional forms of pornography, including online magazine subscriptions and video services (*Playboy*, *Penthouse*, *Hustler*, etc.).

- ○ Photographs and full motion videos from both professional and amateur sources of singles, couples, and groups involved in various sex acts.

- ○ Depiction (both photographic and artistic) of numerous sexual proclivities (bestiality, pedophilia, homosexual relationships, etc.).

- ○ Fictional and nonfictional accounts of sexual encounters, including incest, group sex, bondage, etc.

- ○ Personal ads seeking partners for extramarital affairs, one-night stands, and swingers as well as same-sex and opposite-sex relations.

- ○ Catalogs for sexual devices and clothing.

- ○ Advertisements for pay-for-service organizations ranging from phone sex to escort services.

HATE SPEECH AND RADICAL ACTIVITIES

All manner of supremacist groups are represented online with home pages, chat groups, and bulletin boards for downloading various materials and propaganda. Some examples are:

- ○ Hate speech on a wide array of topics ranging from racial bigotry to the desire for Rush Limbaugh to die a flaming death.

- ○ Information from radical activist groups including the Aryan Nation, Neo-Nazi groups, and state militia organizations.

CompuServe, a large online service provider, recently ran afoul of German authorities for its failure to eliminate Neo-Nazi organizations' information from its service. While the media gave this incident a great deal of coverage, the untold story is that these groups still operate today on CompuServe (and other online services), albeit in a slightly different manner.

VIOLENT AND DESTRUCTIVE MATERIALS

○ Recipes for bombs, booby traps, and other destructive devices

○ Information on drugs and paraphernalia

○ Gang-related activities

The presence of these types of materials was brought home in an especially painful way when a participant at one of my company's recent seminars shared how she and her husband discovered the components of an Oklahoma City–style bomb in their garden shed. Upon further investigation, they learned that their son had found the recipe on the Internet, and he and his friends had purchased the materials at the local hardware store with the intent of "seeing if it worked."

INFORMATION ON CULTS AND OTHER ORGANIZATIONS

○ Witchcraft and related topics

○ Satanic cults and discussion groups

○ Pseudo-religious organizations (Scientology, Krishnas, Branch Davidians, etc.)

In addition to material whose very content is offensive, the opportunity exists online to exploit unsuspecting individuals with potentially dangerous consequences.

Anonymity on the Internet

Unlike face-to-face conversations, interactions on the Internet take place via the keyboard. Consequently, people can masquerade as anything they want to be—old or young, male or female. For many, this can amount to living out a fantasy of beauty or virility. For the most part, it is harmless fun, but consider this situation: Suzie Q., a fourteen-year-old girl, logs on to her normal weekly chat session with other teens from around the world. Tonight, Jane Doe, a *newbie* (someone new to the Internet), is online. Jane is unfamiliar with the Internet, so Suzie helps her out with some instructions about how to act and respond. As part of their conversation, Jane reveals that she is from Suzie's hometown, and a lively chat ensues between the two. Suzie tells Jane about the weekly chat and suggests she join in next week. Over the next few weeks the two meet online and discuss everything from school to boys to homework. Finally, Jane suggests they meet at the local shopping mall for ice cream Friday after school. She tells Suzie what she looks like and where she will be, and Suzie does the same. Innocent enough, right? Well, when Suzie shows up at the mall on Friday to meet Jane, Jane is not a fourteen-year-old girl but a forty-year-old man. Suzie isn't seen or heard from again.

Overstated? Unrealistic? Hardly. Dozens of cases are reported every year where young boys and girls have been lured into compromising situations by pedophiles who win the children's confidence by posing as someone other than themselves. Let's not blame our kids for being kids. Pedophiles are skilled at deception and deceit. They know what children respond to and how to draw them into the open where they can prey on them. The ability for a person to represent him or herself as something completely different on the Internet creates a situation in which pedophiles can prey on children without traditional hurdles of meeting them in person or speaking to them on the telephone.

The potential for anonymity to cause harm isn't limited to children. On a recent *Maury Povich Show*, four couples discussed how their forays on the Internet as someone else led to extramarital affairs that ultimately led to their divorce. Clearly, one of the ethical concerns of the information age will be the social cost.

The potential for adults to prey on children using the Internet is well documented. Numerous cases have been cited in newspapers and periodicals (not to mention the courts) across the nation. Numerous local, state, and federal law enforcement organizations have investigators dedicated to identifying, catching, and prosecuting child pornographers and pedophiles. However, parents should remain the first line of defense between their children and potential danger.

A recent *Readers Digest* article recounted the experiences of the chief of police of Lancaster Township, Pennsylvania. As a result of his interest in computers he began searching the Internet and found himself in a disturbing situation. Because of his work with the abuse of minors, he instantly recognized the "catch words" of those who would pursue minors being used in a chat group in which he was participating. With the help of law enforcement officials from across the country, this officer was able to identify and apprehend the individuals responsible for a child pornography ring and bring these individuals to justice.

SECURITY ON THE INTERNET

Another issue of great concern is the security of personal information on the Internet. If I send email to someone, can it be intercepted and read by others? Can my private chat sessions be monitored by someone else? The answer to both of these questions is that confidentiality is not guaranteed on the Internet anymore than it is when using the U.S. Postal

Service or using the telephone. When we drop a letter in the mail, are we 100 percent guaranteed that it will get delivered to the right place—or at all? When we pick up a portable phone, are we confident that no one is listening in on the same frequency to our conversation? The answer in both cases is obviously no. It is the same on the Internet. No system is absolutely fool-proof. With that said, there are several situations that online users, and particularly parents of teens, should be aware of.

It is one thing to send personal messages whizzing around the world. It is another matter completely to share personal financial information in anything less than a 100 percent secure environment. Even though the fraudulent use of a credit card is not the responsibility of the card holder, many wonder if giving their credit card information over the Internet for commercial transactions is safe or prudent. And with the advent of online banking, a whole new dimension of security must be in place to assure people that their financial transactions are secure.

As part of our seminars, my company spends a great deal of time instructing parents about the appropriate uses of credit card information on the Internet and the warning signs of misuse. When you are establishing your service with a provider, you are frequently asked to provide credit card information for billing purposes. In general, you can assume that doing so is perfectly safe, as the chances that you are connected to someone other than your service provider are slim. Likewise, the chance of someone snatching this data out of the air during transmission is virtually nonexistent. For the most part, this will also be the case when ordering from online catalogs and service companies. Although you should exercise caution to assure yourself that these companies are legitimate providers of goods or services. Most service providers have a method for ordering online and then calling on the telephone to supply credit card information. While this may give the user some level of comfort that a person answered the phone, the transmission of the data is no more secure; in fact, it is less so. The technological aspects of why are unimportant, but suffice it to say that if you will give your credit card information to a catalog shopping service over the phone, you should feel comfortable doing the same thing on the

Internet. However, beware of individuals or "suspect" companies asking for data, especially of a financial nature.

The last area of concern from a security standpoint is the integrity and security of my computer and its data when I am connected to the Internet. Can hackers get into my computer and mess up my hard drive or steal my data? Can my computer get a virus from the Internet? In most cases, the answer is no, but prudent users take precautions to protect their hardware and data from unwanted intrusion. Specific details on how to protect your computer are covered in Chapter 9.

FRAUDULENT ACTIVITIES

Another aspect of the security issue is that of online scams and fraud. The unfamiliarity of most users with the Internet, its uses, and its limitations creates an environment ripe with opportunity for those looking to defraud others. Investment schemes, chain letters, and pyramid schemes are just a few of the many fraudulent activities taking place on the Internet. As Eugene Spafford, Associate Professor of Computer Science at Purdue University, recently noted: "A lot of people committing crimes are taking advantage of the Internet. The nature of the Network enables you to go to an area where none of this is against the law."[1]

Although crime and illegal activity on the Internet are much less prevalent than in real life, some experts expect that to change. "As use of the Internet has expanded, we are finding the Internet being used for more traditional offenses," says Scott Charney, Chief of the Computer Crime Unit in the U.S. Justice Department.[2]

Why the Need for Parental Control

Many people mistakenly believe that objectionable online material is relegated to a few obscure, out-of-the-way locations. In reality, nearly every corner of the online world has at least some access. Even the so-called safe commercial services have areas that cater to this type of information.

A number of issues make control of objectionable material difficult. While no individual issue reigns supreme, they combine to create a formidable foe:

- ◯ No one owns the Internet.

- ◯ No one set of laws binds the Internet's participants.

- ◯ No one regulates the content on the Internet.

- ◯ Technological restrictions would do as much to block good material as bad.

- ◯ What individual or individual's standards should be used as the guide.

How then are we to control these abuses? The two most prominent responses we heard during our research were "The government should pass a law" and "Technology ought to be able to control the flow of this material." In fact, Congress did pass a law as part of the Telecommunication Reform Act of 1996, called the Communications Decency Act. Software companies are making valiant efforts to stem the tide. Despite their efforts, the best solution remains parents getting involved in their kids' online activities.

GOVERNMENT'S INEFFECTIVE CONTROL

During the last two sessions of Congress, several attempts were made to pass legislation that would control inappropriate material on the Internet. The first such attempt was the Exon Amendment, sponsored in 1995 by Senator James Exon. After much debate, this bill was defeated by both houses of congress. In 1996, as part of the larger Telecommunications Reform Act, language was once again introduced. This rider to the Telecommunications Act would ultimately come to be known as the Communications Decency Act and was passed into law in February 1996.

The Communications Decency Act makes it illegal to distribute to children "indecent" or "patently offensive" material over the Internet. Within days, the American Civil Liberties Union, the American Library Association, and others filed challenges on the grounds that the act violated First Amendment rights. Excerpts from these proceedings are included as reference in Appendix E.

The court overturned the law and the Department of Justice has promised appeals to the U.S. Supreme Court if necessary. But the outcome, it is of little consequence, because U.S. laws on pornography end at our nation's shores and there is no recourse for eliminating objectionable material on the Internet that originates overseas. These laws also only deal with pornographic material; they do nothing to stem the tide of other types of material deemed inappropriate for children.

Governments' actions are largely ineffective for several reasons, the most prevalent of which is government's inability to understand the technology. To date, Congressional efforts have focused on classifying the Internet as one of the many current forms of communication available and applying the current laws of that particular medium to the Internet. But what is the Internet? Is it a telephone, a motion picture, a television, a book or magazine, a grocery store?

The telephone, though regulated in terms of service providers, is not regulated with regard to content. After all, do we really want the government censoring what we can and cannot say on the phone?

Television and motion pictures, commonly defined as broadcast media, are subject to regulatory environments that are both governmental- and industry-based. Although the FCC mandates what TV stations can and cannot show, it has made it plain that it wants nothing to do with regulating the Internet. The Motion Picture Rating Association is a self-imposed industry association that established the familiar G, PG-13, R, and X-rated system in response to a governmental threat to regulate the industry. The issue of the success of such a system on the Internet is one of great debate (see sidebar comments).

The right of authors and artists (including photographers) to freely express their artistic viewpoint in literary works has a well-established precedent rooted in the First Amendment to the U.S. Constitution.

The most prevalent forms of pornography on the Internet are pictures and stories that are shielded by the First Amendment's provisions for freedom of speech. How can we declare the very same material we allow to exist in the real world to be illegal in cyberspace?

As a method of both intra- and interstate commerce, the Internet could fall under the jurisdiction of the Treasury Department's Postal regulations or those of the Commerce Department's interstate commerce rules.

The problem lies in the fact that the Internet is unlike any other form of technology used to date. More appropriately, it is similar to virtually all the current forms of technology—and yet dissimilar at the same time. Movies, broadcast, telephone, radio—the Internet is none of these and all of these simultaneously.

A number of less substantive but just as important issues stand in the way of Congress or any other governmental agency regulating the Internet:

○ The length of time required to pass a law, create the rules to be enforced, and ultimately enforce the law is so long that technology changes before the law could be enacted. The result will be a continual string of antiquated laws being applied to technology to which they don't apply. Imagine applying regulations designed to control the objectionable effects of horses on city streets to the automobile.

○ The process of compromise required to gain the required support for a bill to pass both houses of Congress and be signed by the President so dilutes the impact that the result is all too often an ineffective piece of legislation that will not respond to the issues.

○ Most members of Congress do not understand the technology being discussed and lack the staff support to adequately investigate the issues.

○ The issue of what set of moral standards should be used to decide what stays and goes on the Internet is a difficult one. What is offensive to one group may not be offensive to another. The presence of so many special interest groups, each with very powerful lobbies, makes agreement on this topic almost impossible.

Another scheme of control that has received widespread support in Congress and the Internet industry is one of voluntary self-regulation. Such a program would impose an electronic rating on a particular home page based on its level of offensiveness. Using their Internet software, parents could then set the limits that are suitable for their children. There are three fundamental flaws to such a program. First, it only deals with sites on the World Wide Web. Much of the material that parents find objectionable is found in the more spontaneously created chat areas and newsgroups. The material in these areas flow freely on and off each day, making control, much less rating, impossible. Second, who is going to participate? It is hard to imagine the pornographers of the world self-monitoring for the good of our children. Finally, whose standards will we use to determine how a site should be rated?

Accountability for what children are exposed to ultimately rests with parents. We must realize that our society and the Internet will always contend with individuals with little or no moral character, and the government—no matter how hard it tries—can never be our defender against all things distasteful.

INABILITY OF TECHNOLOGY TO CONTROL CONTENT

In today's ever-expanding online universe, computer users can explore an array of topics—including those aimed at adults only. In fact, the very structure that has allowed the Internet to grow so rapidly, with such valuable information has also allowed less appropriate material to grow as well. Almost like growing a new lawn, a few weeds are cast among a lot of good seed.

Given the sophistication of the technology used to operate the Internet, it would seem to most people that eliminating inappropriate material should be a relatively simple thing. In fact, it is quite the opposite. The very sophistication of the technology that makes the Internet such a rapid communication tool effectively prevents the censorship of content transmitted. A quick review of how information is accessed on the Internet will help to clarify why this is so.

You probably begin by signing onto an Internet Service Provider (ISP) via telephone lines. The ISP then interconnects to all the other computers of the Internet a high-speed digital "backbone" which is nothing more than a network of telephone lines dedicated to data transmisssion for the Internet. When you request information or access a home page, the *host computer*, or computer where the information resides, will send the requested information using the most efficient route available at the nanosecond you requested the information. That route may go through any number of states or even countries, regardless of where the request originated. On its travels, the information may go through six computers—or six thousand. And more importantly, if you sent the same request just one minute later, the chances are it would take a completely different route before the information eventually came back to your computer. One last bit of information is very important. A whole message may not all travel the same route! If technology is to intercept "the bad stuff," which one of the many computers is supposed to accomplish that task?

Numerous suggestions have been made to hold service providers accountable for the materials they allow to be transmitted on their services. After all, every user has to sign on through a unique service provider, right? Ignoring for a moment the fact that service providers outside the United States would not be subject to such laws, this scheme is as impractical as the first. Service providers are in the technological business of connecting computers, not unlike the phone company is responsible for connecting phones. While theoretically these companies could be made to examine every online "conversation," it is no more practical to do so than it would be to listen to every one of the billions of telephone conversations that occur each day. Even if the ability were there to accomplish this Herculean feat, do we really want a third party determining what we can and cannot say via the telephone lines?

The final hurdle standing in the way of either commercial service providers or Internet service providers playing a watchdog role is one of economics. The business of being a service provider is based on having large numbers of users to defray the cost of equipment and phone service costs. Essentially, it is a business of very narrow margins. The number of people required to "watch" each and every conversation would be astronomical and the cost prohibitive. To put these pieces in place would drive the cost of service so high as to create natural limits as to who could use the Internet rather than creating an international communication tool inexpensive enough for all to use.

> The courts have also played a role in removing the incentive for service providers to act as censors. A recent court ruling held that if a service provider holds itself out as monitoring and controlling the type of information available on its service, the public has the right to rely on that assertion and hold the service liable if damaging material is not censored. In today's litigious society, services are safer by refusing to play any censorship role than to risk exposure for not catching every incident.

The last technological opportunity to manage access to unwanted material is to remove the server providing the material from the Internet. Unfortunately, in doing so, any material of redeeming value would also no longer be available—the epitome of throwing the baby out with the bath water.

Parents: The Only Viable Option

The presence of adult material shouldn't deter you from going online, but you need to be aware that it exists and know how to control or avoid those areas. As parents, we must exercise control over these areas in cyberspace just as we would in real life through education, guidance, instruction, and example.

Our schools do a great job of regulating online time within the school but have no control over what transpires outside of the school building. As unlimited Internet access for children grows at astronomical rates in homes and libraries, there will be no control without parental control. Kids don't purchase computers, modems, and Internet access accounts; parents do. The Internet is a tool, and parents must exercise the same degree of caution that they would if they allowed their children to use any other inherently dangerous tool. What responsible parent would purchase a handgun and allow their children to use it without supervision or instruction?

Parents, if you had any doubts as to your role when you picked this book up, I hope I have eliminated them. *You* are the only ones who are adequately equipped to decide who, what, when, where, and how much.

THE PARENTAL ACTION MATRIX

As we address the issues of what parents can do to create a suitable environment for their children, we will employ a matrix of sorts that is both age- and skill-based. By simply finding your child's attributes, you can find what actions you should take in your home. Ironically, the younger and less knowledgeable your children are, the greater your range of options. For older children who are more independent and less responsive to parental involvement, the best assurances are the software products available on the market. A visual depiction of this matrix is on the facing page

The various interventions show on the matrix are detailed in Chapters 6 to 8, following more detailed discussion of selecting a service provider and what hardware you will require to "get on the net."

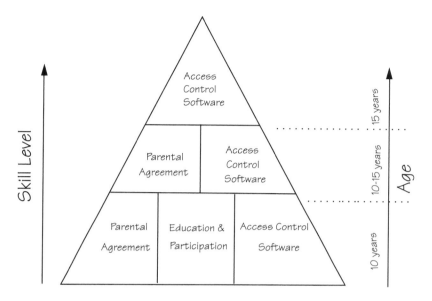

Figure 2.1 Parental Action Matrix.

FOOTNOTES

[1] PC Novice; Special Reprint "Guide to Going Online," December 1995

[2] PC Novice; Special Reprint "Guide to Going Online," December 1995

The Online World:

What You Should Know About the Internet and Commercial Online Services

Imagine a place that is open 24 hours a day, 365 days a year. A place to meet people, share ideas and experiences, ask questions, give advice, look for a job or a mate. Imagine the information resources of thousands of universities, government agencies and researchers at your fingertips. Imagine shopping malls that never close, where you can shop for everything from automobiles to zircons. A place of adventure and romance, wealth and privilege. Welcome to Cyberspace, the final frontier.

But is it a frontier? Cyberspace is not really a place; it has no limits, no borders, and no defined boundaries. And yet it is a place where you can go to meet people, get information, communicate, learn, and explore. In the words of Nicole Stenger's essay in *Cyberspace: First Steps*,[1] "Cyberspace is the place in the mind where those who connect to each other electronically share their thoughts and feelings."

There are many ways to establish this electronic connection to share or obtain information. The two most common are commercial service providers (CSPs) like CompuServe, America Online, and Prodigy; and Internet Service Providers (ISPs).

Commercial Service Providers

If you are an online beginner, or *newbie*, the commercial service providers are a great way to get your feet wet. They all make getting online very easy. All you need is a computer, a modem, and one of the free diskettes you may have received in the mail, a monthly publication, or even shrink-wrapped with Sunday's newspaper.

Simply insert the disk in your computer's floppy drive, answer the questions that appear on the screen, and you are closer than half a dozen mouse "clicks" to that familiar high-pitched squeal as the modem logs on. Then voilá... you have stepped into Cyberspace!

Once online, you will find places to have private and group conversations, to be a part of lively online discussions with nationally known experts, to download shareware programs from other users, to play online games, to browse through the articles of hundreds of periodicals and online magazines, to go on a shopping spree, to make flight or hotel reservations, and to track your investments with the latest stock market quotes and investment advice. In short, many of the services you expect from the Internet plus a cadre of value-added services unique to the particular commercial service to which you subscribe.

However, commercial service providers are not the Internet. Although virtually all commercial services now offer access to the Internet, they all started as—and remain—some form of "intranet." Like the local area networks (LANs) many of us are familiar with in corporations, these providers create a single network where registered users can exchange information and data with other subscribers to the same service. For example, a CompuServe user could not "join" an America Online chat room or exchange information with an America Online subscriber and vice versa.

This stand-alone aspect is a legacy of the time when commercial entities were not allowed to access the Internet. Virtually all the commercial providers began as commercial ventures with the goal of creating a worldwide network of users able to connect to one another without the use of the Internet, which at the time was not available to commercial services. The result is a number of independent companies, each owned by a corporation with shareholders, corporate officers, CEOs, and employees. Those employees spend millions of dollars each year developing new products, billing, accounting, operating the huge mainframe computers that support the network, and, last of all, marketing. Users pay a monthly fee of approximately $10 plus access fees of about $2.50 to $3 per hour to access these networks, and in return they receive access to other users of the same network.

CompuServe is the oldest of the commercial service providers. It began in 1969, when a Columbus, Ohio, insurance company bought much more computing power than it needed and then sought to sell excess capacity to the general public to offset costs. CompuServe has grown to more than three million users spanning the globe. These users enjoy 120 basic services for a monthly fee as well and special optional services for which additional charges are levied.

CompuServe is used almost exclusively for business and research. Numerous professional organizations maintain forums (CompuServe's electronic bulletin boards) and chat areas dedicated to specific topics or professions.

Prodigy and America Online target families, students, and casual users. This consumer focus, combined with incredible marketing savvy has made America Online the fastest growing CSP with more than five million users at the time of this writing. Each of the major national online services has distinct advantages and disadvantages that are discussed in detail in Chapter 5.

Perhaps the most important fact is that all commercial providers now provide access to the Internet as a kind of middle man. This allows users to simultaneously use the provider's various value-added services and access the vast information resources of the Internet. This access is a relatively recent occurrence, and it has generated an increasing amount of discussion in the industry about the long-term viability of commercial services. Many of the services once offered only by commercial providers for a fee are now offered via the Internet for free. Underscoring these discussions about the limited resources of commercial services and the Internet are the recent agreements by America Online, CompuServe, Prodigy, and Netscape to support the latter's Internet browser—the world's most popular way of exploring the Internet. This continued blurring of service offerings has only served to muddy the waters and has made differentiation difficult on all points except price. Commercial service providers may someday disappear but until ISPs make access easier, commercial service providers will remain one of the best ways for new users to get their feet wet.

Internet Service Providers

While some users connect to the Internet through schools or work and many others use a commercial service provider's gateway, the best way to obtain fast and less expensive online access is through a local or national Internet service provider. Most service providers charge a fee for Internet access on a monthly, hourly, or annual basis, or on a combination of hourly charges and monthly or annual fees. The actual fees will depend on the type of account, they are typically approximately $1 per hour, up to a cap of $10 to $30 per month. After that, usage is unlimited with no additional charges. Simply check the business section of your local newspaper to locate a service provider in your area, and see Chapter 5 for a detailed discussion of considerations when choosing a service provider. A drawback to most ISPs is that they offer access only to the Internet, and getting online is often more difficult than the "foolproof" environment commercial service providers offer. However, there is an increasing trend toward local and national service providers developing graphical "front-end" software that puts a variety of Internet services only a mouse click away.

A growing number of providers are giving access to schools, churches, libraries, and communities at no charge. There are also Internet service providers called *FreeNets*, which are usually supported by donations of equipment from computer and telecommunications companies and operated by volunteers. Although most do not offer all the services of the local ISP, there is not a more economical way to get online. If you are a member of a not-for-profit organization, check with local computer stores or computer user groups to determine whether such an organization is available to you.

The Internet

While the argument rages on in the industry about the viability of commercial services, it is clear that regardless of how you enter the online world, your ultimate destination is the Internet. Industry estimates put more than 30 million users on the Internet worldwide—and this number is growing at an astonishing 10% per month, with estimates of more than 100 million users by the turn of the century. In contrast, the largest of the commercial services, America Online, has only 5 million users. Clearly, the lure to the Internet is great, regardless of how you get there.

Where commercial online services represent a single network of users all interconnected, the Internet is a network of networks that allows greatly expanded access to a much wider array of information. Some 25,000 interconnected networks made up of several hundred thousand host computers or servers span the globe, ready to exchange information, data, games, and other entertainment and to allow you to connect to people all over the world. Commercial online services such as America Online and CompuServe offer a wide range of special-interest bulletin boards and chat groups on a wide array of topics. However, the Internet offers access to thousands of similar newsgroups and mailing lists on topics that range from "Kite Ballet" to the Bolshoi and from witchcraft to Windows 95.

You can also browse the world's largest library. The Internet's online library is open 24 hours every day and lets you check out as many books, games, programs, videos, and audio tapes as you want for free. Search the Library of Congress card catalog or the local public library's online catalog in most major cities, or thumb through millions of pages of U.S. government writings from the comfort of your computer chair.

There are dozens of services available on the Internet, but these five are the most popular:

○ **email**—allows messages to be sent worldwide in minutes without cost (beyond the cost of connection).

○ **Usenet Newsgroups**—allows individuals of mutual interests to exchange information on electronic bulletin boards.

○ **Internet Relay Chat**—individuals can participate in live, interactive discussions via the keyboard, on any of thousands of topics, and if one doesn't suit you, you can start your own.

○ **File Transfer Protocol (FTP) sites**—where dozens of freeware and shareware programs are available at little or no cost; many software developers also use FTP sites to make upgrades and patches available to users.

○ **The World Wide Web**—A graphical user interface to the text-based Internet.

Developed in 1992 by a group of Swiss scientists, the World Wide Web (the Web for short) has been primarily responsible for the explosion of Internet users in the past several years. Logging on to the Internet and using a software product called a *browser,* users point and click their way through the thousands of online shopping malls, art and science museums, bookstores, corporate advertisements, and personal home pages. Imagine the splendor of *National Geographic* coming to life on your screen, complete not only with the still photographs we are accustomed to but also with sound and video clips, and you will start to see why to experience the World Wide Web is to love it.

An additional attraction is that once connected, most of the services available on the Internet are free of charge.

A LITTLE HISTORY

To give a feeling for the relative newness of the Internet and the associated commercial service providers, Figure 3.1 depicts the evolution of the Internet, from its modest beginnings in the late 1960s to today.

The Internet was conceived in 1969 when a group of Defense Department researchers working at four different institutions decided to link their computers via telephone wires so they could "talk" with one another about the various projects they were working on. Thus the computers at UCLA, Stanford Research Institute, the University of Utah, and the University of California–Santa Barbara were linked into what would become known as *ARPAnet*, the Defense Department's Advanced Research Projects Agency network.

The network was a great idea, and it grew rapidly. In three short years, more than 50 universities and military agencies were linked via telephone lines to ARPAnet. Throughout the 1970s, the use of computer networks expanded, and other computer networks began appearing around the country and the world. By 1983, enough other networks had joined ARPAnet that the military research people thought they would be better off with their own network, and the military and educational networks diverged. At about the same time, the National Science Foundation (NSF) built a series of supercomputer centers connected with high-speed long-distance lines. The NSFnet, as this network would come to be known, would eventually replace the ARPAnet as managers and form the backbone of the Internet. By 1991, so many universities, research laboratories, and high-tech companies had created computer networks that were joined to the NSFnet that the federal government made it known the network's backbone would no longer be limited to use in research.

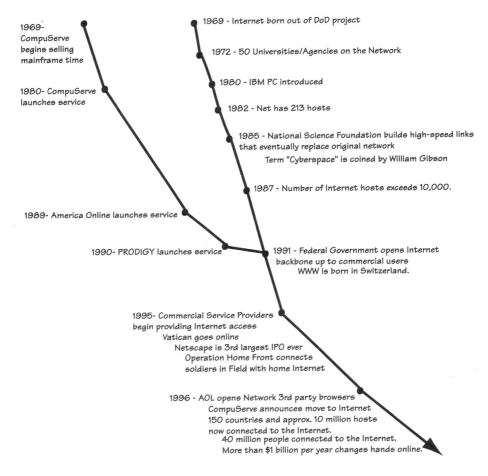

1969- CompuServe begins selling mainframe time

1980- CompuServe launches service

1989- America Online launches service

1990- PRODIGY launches service

1995- Commercial Service Providers begin providing Internet access
Vatican goes online
Netscape is 3rd largest IPO ever
Operation Home Front connects soldiers in Field with home Internet

1996 - AOL opens Network 3rd party browsers
CompuServe announces move to Internet
150 countries and approx. 10 million hosts now connected to the Internet.
40 million people connected to the Internet.
More than $1 billion per year changes hands online.

1969 - Internet born out of DoD project

1972 - 50 Universities/Agencies on the Network

1980 - IBM PC introduced

1982 - Net has 213 hosts

1985 - National Science Foundation builds high-speed links that eventually replace original network
Term "Cyberspace" is coined by William Gibson

1987 - Number of Internet hosts exceeds 10,000.

1991 - Federal Government opens Internet backbone up to commercial users
WWW is born in Switzerland.

Figure 3.1 A history of online services.

Throughout the late 1970s and 1980s numerous governmental agencies created networks that ultimately became part of the Internet. This trend has intensified over the past few years to where almost every federal and state agency has some sort of presence on the Internet. A partial list of those agencies follows:

The Federal Reserve Board
The Census
Congressional Directory
Congressional Quarterly
Department of Agriculture Extension Service
Department of Commerce
Department of Education
Department of Health and Human Services
Department of Housing and Urban Development
Department of Justice
Environmental Protection Agency
Federal Communications Commission
House of Representatives
The Library of Congress (MARVEL)
National Archives and Records
Senate
Social Security Administration
Copyright Office
Patent and Trademark Office
Central Intelligence Agency
Consumer Information Center
The Entire U.S. Government on the Web

Federal Register

SEC EDGAR Database

The Small Business Administration

General Services Administration (GSA)

Internal Revenue Service

The White House

This opened the door for numerous commercial networks to become part of the Internet. Today the Internet is used primarily by academics, office workers, and consumers, who send text, still photographs, sound, and video images across the Internet.

WHAT IS THE INTERNET?

The researchers who created the Internet needed a way to safely store and communicate sensitive government information in the event of a nuclear war. The solution was a network that lacked a central computer to store its billions of bytes of information or direct the actions of remote computers. Each *node* or site on the network would stand alone but was also interconnected to the others so that destruction of one (in the event of a nuclear attack) would not prevent the free interchange of information or destroy the data stored on the other sites. Today, the result is a decentralized network with data stored on each of the thousands of computers that make up the network and speak a common language. The *Internet,* then, is a network of networks, each interconnected so that the network is redundant. This means that if a particular computer was to break, the rest of the computers connected through that network could use any number of other connections to maintain their links to the Internet.

To visualize the power of the Internet, imagine for a moment that every phone throughout the world was replaced by a computer and that each of these computers could "talk" to each other. This very simple analogy, though not factually accurate, does represent the power of the Internet and the reach it may soon have.

In addition to a communication role, each of the hundreds of thousands of Internet servers resembles a mini-library. Each server maintains its own information, cataloging that information, and deciding what stays and what goes. Although this analogy of a library is a good one, it is incorrect because there is no "card catalog" for the Internet. A more accurate picture would be that of a book warehouse, where the various collections of each contributing family are stored without a reference as to what is in the collection. To make finding a particular volume or topic easier and far less intimidating, there are numerous programs called *search engines* that allow us to search the vast depths of these collections by simply typing in the word or words we are looking for and hitting the **Enter** key. Figure 3.2 shows the result of a search on the Internet. You can see that the Internet is not only a tool with the potential to tremendously speed communication but also to store vast amounts of data and make that information available to millions of people worldwide.

Figure 3.2 Sample outcome of a WebCrawler search.

> ### SEARCH ENGINES
>
> A *search engine* is a program used to locate a particular site or sites on the Internet based on Boolean Logic search methods in which desired terms are linked with connectors (*and, or, not*) to define a the search (e.g., garden *and* flowers *not* vegetables). A few of the most common search engines are WebCrawler, Lycos, and Yahoo.

How the Internet Works

So how does the Internet accomplish this seemingly impossible task? To illustrate the mind-boggling complexity of the Internet, let's use the example of an email message sent from Los Angeles to New York.

Most of the discussion in this section applies to both commercial service providers and the Internet. However, it is useful to remember that while the technology works identically, commercial service providers maintain completely separate networks that do not interconnect with the Internet. Therefore, to gain access to the Internet, commercial service provider users must use a *gateway,* or a toll booth to the Internet, and pay hourly usage fees for that access that are separate and added to those of the commercial service providers.

The journey begins for our email message when we compose it on our computer. This is typically done in an email program, but it could just as easily be done in any one of a number of word processing programs and then pasted into an email program. We then ask the computer to dial the Internet using a modem. For more information on modems, see Chapter 4. For now, let's just say that the modem turns the words and letters on our screen into a message that is capable of speeding down the telephone wires to its destination, where another modem receives it and turns it back into words and letters on the recipient's screen. When the computer is told to send the message, the modem converts the message to a series of digital signals that are sent to an Internet server.

Literally millions of email messages are sent each minute worldwide. To facilitate this vast amount of traffic, the information traveling on the Internet must conform to a series of traffic laws, or *protocols*. The best way to understand these protocols is to think of each one as a layer that builds on the previous one. Compliance with these traffic laws allows your data to flow smoothly from one computer to the next without interruption.

The first layer is actually two protocols that make up the common language that all networks connected to the Internet share—*Transmission Control Protocol/Internet Protocol (TCP/IP)*. To illustrate the role of TCP/IP, imagine a book being sent through the post office—one page at a time. Each page would be inserted into an envelope, addressed, and mailed. Each page would hopefully arrive at its destination, but this would happen over different routes and in no specific order. Finally, the recipient would recompile the book using page numbers and then request that any damaged or missing pages be copied and sent again so they could be inserted to complete the book.

Just like our book, information sent via the Internet is broken up into packets, or *datagrams,* that can be sent via telephone lines, cable, or satellite uplinks. Internet Protocol allows a single message to be broken into hundreds or thousands of individual packets that will be sent to their destination via an infinite number of routes and may or may not arrive in order or maybe not at all! IP addresses each packet so that any computer on the network can forward it to another computer closer to the destination. IP also routes each packet along the most efficient route, available at the time and while these routes are seldom the most logical they do make the best use of the hundreds of thousands of computers on the network. However, like the post office, once the message is sent, IP has no way of making sure the packet arrives intact or at all.

This is where Transmission Control Protocol takes over. TCP's purpose is to ensure reliable transmissions of messages across the Internet. TCP examines each IP packet to make sure it was not damaged during transmission. It also resequences the packets from whatever order they were received in into their original order. Finally, TCP requests that any missing or damaged packets be re-sent and then inserts them in the proper places.

Many other protocols may also affect our work, depending on the activity. File Transfer Protocol standardizes the way files are sent from one computer to another. Network News Transmission Protocol (NNTP) is used to transmit messages from Usenet newsgroups. Returning to our email example, Simple Mail Transfer Protocol (SMTP) establishes the specific steps that one computer must take to connect to another computer to transmit the message to its next stop.

All right, we have composed and sent our email message and our computer has applied the appropriate protocols. What happens next? Similar to a letter sent via the U.S. Postal Service, your message will travel through several Internet post offices along the way, each sorting, forwarding and distributing the email messages it receives. Each message goes to a *router,* or smart link, that sends the message through high-speed telephone lines to the Internet. The router reads the address on each data packet and decides how it should proceed to its final destination. Routers also evaluate how busy a particular network is and can send data on an alternate route to avoid traffic jams.

On its way down the information superhighway, a message receives roadside assistance from repeaters, hubs, bridges, and gateways. Each plays a specific role, ensuring that your message arrives in its original form. *Repeaters* super charge, or *amplify,* the digital signal as it starts to slow down and then whip it to its next destination. *Hubs* are the interchanges of the information highway; they act as communication links between networks. A single message could conceivably go through dozens of hubs before reaching it destination. *Bridges* connect the local area networks on the network, allowing data to go from LAN to LAN without interruption. Finally, gateways allow different types of networks to talk to each other by acting as translators. Gateways are particularly important to users of commercial online services, because they allow them to access the Internet to send mail and use other Internet services. Which brings us to our final point—how does all this differ for commercial online services?

Information transfer on a commercial service provider is much the same as on the Internet, except that each commercial service provider uses a proprietary set of protocols unique to that service. Users dial in to a local number and log onto a *node* (an endpoint on the network associated with a local phone number to avoid long-distance charges) of the commercial service provider network. Using a special communications protocol, your computer is allowed to "talk" to the service provider's mainframe computer and transmit data by dividing information into packets, sending and sorting those packets just as TCP/IP does on the Internet.

The only exception to this routine happens when commercial service users want to access the Internet to send email, surf the World Wide Web or access any of the other Internet services. For commercial service users to access these services, communications must go through an additional step to convert the proprietary protocols of the service providers to those of the Internet. This is all done behind the scenes through a conversion processor attached to the commercial service provider's mainframe computer.

None of the information contained in this chapter is necessary to use an online service, any more than a thorough understanding of your car's engine is required to drive down the highway. However, a little understanding of how the process works will go a long way toward helping you make the right decision when it comes to selecting a service provider, determining how to best control online material, and creating a "cyber-safe" environment for your home.

FOOTNOTES

[1]*Cyberspace: First Steps*, Michael Benedikt, MIT Press, 1991.

Hardware You Will Need to Access the Internet

Accessing online services can be accomplished from virtually anywhere assuming that you have four things: a computer, a modem, a phone connection, and an Internet service provider. The first three are covered in detail in this chapter. The fourth is not a hardware issue at all but rather is a company or organization whose computer your modem dials up that allows you to connect to the Internet. It is actually the provider's equipment your modem dials when you click on your Internet's software icon to log on.

A few of the most popular online and internet service providers are America Online, CompuServe, Prodigy and Microsoft Network (MSN), Pipeline USA, and NETCOM. Though many of the services these companies offer are identical, each has their own advantages and disadvantages. An in-depth discussion of how to choose a service provider based on your needs can be found in Chapter 5.

Selecting a computer or recommending one brand or type over another is beyond the scope of this book. However, what type of hardware you ultimately select will greatly affect your online performance and therefore some discussion is appropriate. In addition to providing a general outline of what particular types of computers do, detailed discussion of the other components that will impact what online services you ultimately utilize can be found in the rest of this chapter.

What Kind of Computer Do I Need?

For the purposes of online connection, one computer looks pretty much like another whether it is an Apple, an IBM, or one of the many IBM-compatible brands available on the market today. In my role as an educator, I am often people's first introduction to the Internet so we are often asked questions like: How fast does my computer have to be? How much memory do I need? and How much RAM do I need? My response to these questions in most cases is: If you have a computer that works, a modem, and a phone line you can access the Internet.

That being said, if what you want to do is access the World Wide Web and all its graphical images as well as audio and video programs, you will need a faster, more expensive computer using a Windows operating system equipped with enhanced video and audio cards or a Macintosh. But if your goal is to utilize the Internet for research and access to text-only areas your current computer may be more than adequate.

Your ability to utilize online services will be much more dependent on your operating system (Windows, Windows 95, DOS, or Apple System 7), peripheral cards (sound and video), and your modem than the speed of your computer. These are the components that will determine whether you can access the graphical portions of the Internet. The text portions of the Internet are available to even the oldest Mac SE or 286 IBM-compatible computer.

To achieve the most complete use of online services you will need a 386, or better IBM or compatible processor, with VGA or better video output; a mouse; and a sound card. For Macintosh users, a Mac IILC with a 68020 Processor or better, is the minimum requirement. These Macs already support both video and sound, so no additional equipment is required, other than a modem. It goes without saying that faster more powerful computers will be able to do more. However, don't let the limitation of your current hardware configuration stop you from trying only those services that are available to you, given your current equipment.

Commercial service providers all require machines with graphical capabilities as a minimum to access their services. More detailed discussion of the particular requirements of each service can be found in Chapter 5.

Table 4.1 depicts the most common processor speeds and typical configurations and the services available online given that configuration. Obviously, to depict all combinations would be impractical but by first picking the processor with which your machine is equipped and then determining the operating environment and output mechanisms available for your specific machine, you should be able to determine what limitations your current equipment may pose to online access.

If you are making your first computer purchase, which type of machine you buy is really a question of personal choice. Apple's release of the Power Macs and Microsoft's Windows 95 operating system have greatly blurred the differences between operating platforms. Macs remain slightly easier to use and are the norm in secondary schools, but they cost a little bit more and are less prevalent in the market. The result is peripherals (printers, modems, disk drives, etc.) that are slightly more expensive and a selection of software titles that is more limited than those available to IBM-compatible users.

Table 4.1 Internet services available using common processor speeds and configuration.

	PROCESSOR	MODEM SPEED	OUTPUT DEVICES	AVAILABLE INTERNET SERVICES
DOS/ Windows	286	1200 bps 9600bps	Video: CGA/EGA/VGA Sound: None	Gopher Telnet WAIS
	386	4800 bps 9600 bps	Video: VGA/SVGA Sound: None	Gopher/ Telnet WAIS/IRC Chat/FTP Newsgroups/WWW
	486	9600 bps 28.8 Kbps	Video: VGA/SVGA Sound: 16-bit Sound Card	Gopher/ Telnet WAIS/IRC Chat/FTP Newsgroups/WWW
	Pentium	14.4 Kbps 28.8 Kbps	Video: SVGA Sound: 16-bit Sound Card	Gopher/ Telnet WAIS/IRC Chat/FTP Newsgroups/WWW
Macintosh	68020	1200 bps 9600bps	Video: Std.(Built-in) Sound: None	Gopher Telnet WAIS
	68030/40	9600 bps 28.8 Kbps	Video: Std. Or RGB Color Sound Std	Gopher/ Telnet WAIS/IRC Chat/FTP Newsgroups/WWW
	PowerMac	14.4 Kbps 28.8 Kbps	Video: Std. Sound Std.	Gopher/ Telnet WAIS/IRC Chat/FTP

IBM-compatibles on the other hand are not as intuitive to set up or use even with the Windows 95 operating environment. However, they outsell Macs approximately 10 to 1 and are still the mainstay of businesses around the world. The shear number of competing manufacturers makes used machines readily available and keep the prices of new machines very competitive. The same is also true for peripherals and software.

Multimedia packages are available from virtually every computer manufacturer today. They come complete with computer, CD-ROM, hard drive, sound and video cards, stereo speakers, operating software, and pre-installed software packages that make the machines simple to set up. The distinct advantage to these packages is first of all price and second the elimination of any hardware or software conflicts encountered as part of the setup procedure because the machines are preconfigured before shipping.

Regardless of what type of computer you ultimately decide on, either will allow you access to the online world and the many exciting adventures that await you there.

Choosing and Using Modems

No other product is as central to going online as the modem. However, selecting a modem is a bit like a trip to the candy store. How do you choose the right modem for your equipment and your needs? How do you compare performance? Which features are worth having? How much should you pay? At first glance there are so many colors and shapes and sizes and flavors—but it is really a question of personal choice. First, let's review the basics (see Figure 4.1).

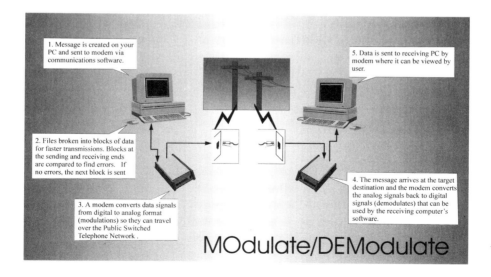

Figure 4.1 *Modem basics.*

Modem stands for MOdulator-DEModulator and is nothing more than a translator between the computer and the telephone system. The modem allows your computer to talk to another by changing what you type (the digital signals of computer language) into the analog signals a telephone transmits. The modem plugs into the phone line between the telephone jack in the wall and your current handset and attaches to one of your computer's COM ports or in the case of a Macintosh plugs into the jack with a phone icon above it. Once the message is sent, the analog signal goes to another modem at the receiving end that is using the same protocol and communications parameters that you are to convert the analog signal back to digital to display the message on the receiving computer's screen. Both protocols and communication parameters will be discussed later, but think of them as the language a computer speaks. Even if you were able to make a phone call to someone in Paris, it would be difficult to have a conversation if you didn't speak French or they English. It is the same with computers but "speaking French" is as easy a flipping a switch to the correct protocol.

If your computer did not come with a modem or if your are in the market for a faster one, the following section may be of interest. If your modem came preconfigured or you are already online, you may want to skip this section and go directly to Chapter 5.

Baud Rate and V Numbers

According to Odyssey Homefront, a national home market survey for personal computers, approximately half of the PCs in U.S. homes have modems. Modems have become so commonplace that most new multimedia computers sold include an internal modem as part of the standard package. These modems are usually quite fast (14.4 or 28.8Kbps) and are preconfigured for immediate use. All that is required of the user is to plug a phone line into a wall jack and into the back of the computer.

Modems come in different modulation speeds that are measured in *bits per second (bps)*. This is often referred to as the baud rate of a modem, and while this is not technically correct, the two are often used interchangeably. For many years, 2400bps modems were the norm, but now the prices of higher-speed modems dropped to the point that today either 28.8Kbps or 14.4Kbps (kilobits per second) are considered the norm, though many 9600bps modems are still in operation.

> To give you some sense of the difference in speed, it would take about 53 days to transfer the contents of a CD-ROM from one computer to another at a rate of 1200bps. Using a 28.8Kbps modem (V.34 standard) the same task would be executed over twenty-five times faster. It is useful to point our however, that not all service providers or computers allow communication at this rate. Many services still run at a maximum speed of 9600 baud and in older PCs the serial port connection limits data transfer to a maximum of 9600 baud while new serial port cards give speeds of up to 57600 baud. Therefore, modems operating at up to 14400 baud (V.32), which are considerably cheaper than the faster modems, may in practice be equally fast.

In fact, the price differential between 2400bps and 14.4Kbps is so slight as to make purchasing anything less than 14.4Kbps impractical. To insure that all modems throughout the world are capable of "talking" to each other, an organization of the United Nations is establishing standards to which all modems must conform. These standards are indicated with "vee" numbers. The standard for 9600bps modems is *V.32*, while the standard for 14.4Kbps is *V.32bis*. The standard for 28.8Kbps is *V.34*. One other "vee" number you may encounter is *V.42* or *V.42bis*. This is an error-correcting and data compression algorithm that allows much higher rates of data transmission. For instance, a V.42 (14.4Kbps) modem is capable of transmitting at 57.6Kbps, and a V.42bis (28.8Kbps) modem can attain speeds of as high as 115.2Kbps.

INTERNAL OR EXTERNAL

Modems are either internal—a card is inserted into a slot inside your computer—or external, they come in a stand-alone box. *Internal modems* are typically less expensive, require no cabling other than from the phone cable and can, in some cases , outperform an external model of a similar speed rating. *External modems* can be used with different computers and allow ease of monitoring the state of your online connection. A third alternative available for laptops or notebook computers is the *PCMCIA card modem*. These modems are about the size of two credit cards stacked on top of each other and have a pop-out jack to connect the phone line. Unfortunately, like most things electronic, small size means big dollars and you can expect to pay almost twice as much for these modems as you would for a desktop model.

COMPRESSION AND ERROR CORRECTION

Most newer modems have error correction and data compression functions built into them. *Data compression* reduces the overall size of the file being transferred and improves the effective transfer speed thus decreasing the time required to be online. *Error correction* deals with unwanted changes in the transferring data that are caused by phone line interference and automatically replaces the damaged data with corrected data The complexity of what these features do is masked by the fact that it happens automatically and are well worth a few extra dollars to eliminate a great number of headaches you might otherwise encounter. However be advised that these features will only be implemented when you are connected with a similarly equipped modem.

CABLES

Check whether the modem you are thinking of buying comes with connecting cables, and if it does, check that they are the correct ones for your computer. If you want to use the modem on more than one type of computer it is likely that you will require more than one set of cables. If you are in doubt, just ask the sales representative where you buy your modem.

SOFTWARE

Modems need software to make them work. Most modems come with communications software included that may be very useful but may not be the one you want to use. Try the software that comes with your modem and with your operating system. If neither of these suits your needs, computer magazines print reviews of communications packages that should lead you to one that will.

FAX CAPABILITY

It is well worth considering a combined modem and fax unit that will allow you to send both computer data and faxes. Sending a fax directly from your computer is much simpler since there is no need to print out a document and then manually feed it into a fax machine. Fax software automatically converts the file to a fax document, dials the appropriate telephone fax number, sends the document, and hangs up when finished. In most cases, it will also allow you to receive and print faxes as long as your computer and modem are switched on and connected to the phone line.

Our company frequently receives calls from frustrated users who cannot receive faxes even though the phone is ringing. In fifty percent of these cases the problem is either that they have not plugged their phone line into their modem or the modem is turned off, preventing the computer from answering the phone.

CONFIGURING YOUR SYSTEM: COMMUNICATION PARAMETERS

In addition to the information discussed in this section, you may be asked for information about your service provider when configuring your hardware. Check the service providers start up documentation for this information if necessary. In most cases you will also be prompted for this information when you install your service provider's software.

For two modems to communicate smoothly, they need to be set to the same communication parameters, or settings. The advent of plug and play peripherals and auto hardware recognition as part of Windows 95 have made the set up of modems much simpler than in the past though some tweaking may still be necessary to have fax communication software, online access software, dialers and the like all work together.

The following is a brief overview of the things you must do when configuring your modem to talk to another whether you are going online or communicating with your computer at the office. There is no way to foresee all the possible combinations of problems people will face but in general the setup is very simple. Finally, nothing in this section is meant to supersede or replace the very detailed instructions you received with your equipment. Should you have any questions consult the users manual or phone the technical assistance number for the equipment manufacturer.

After selecting a service provider (see Chapter 5), you will need to configure your modem to operate using the same parameters as the service provider. To accomplish this, there are six categories of information you will need:

○ Speed or bps rate

○ Data bits

○ Parity

○ Stop bits

○ Duplex

○ Terminal emulation

Descriptions of what each of these represent are listed below. To find out the particular settings for the online service you have selected, check the Getting Started or Set Up sections of the documentation they provided in your starter kit. If you don't find the information there, call the customer services number your service provided you and ask a service representative.

Note Configuring your modem is probably the most complex thing you will do to get online but I think you will agree by the end of this chapter, that if this is the most complex thing you have to do, anybody can get online.

Data bits indicate the size of each piece of data being transmitted. This number will usually have a value of either seven or eight.

Parity is a simple form of error checking. With even parity, the character must have an even number to be deemed error-free by the receiving modem. With odd parity, the character must have an odd number. Parity is only a very rudimentary form of error correction so it is often done away with.

Stop bits mark the end of a character. There is usually only one stop bit though there can be two.

Duplex determines how the keystrokes you type appear on the screen. At *half duplex,* the keystrokes appear as a direct result of your typing them. At *full duplex,* they appear as a result of the receiving modem echoing the keystroke back to indicate it has been received.

Terminal emulation matches your system with the system to which you are connecting. The idea is that your PC will act like a particular type of terminal while it is connected to another computer such as a mainframe or server.

To check or change the communications parameters you are currently using:

○ Open your communications package by double-clicking the mouse on the program icon. You will probably find this either on your desktop or in the folder set up for your online service. If you are using a commercial service provider for access, launch the application itself.

○ Click on the **Configure** or **Setup** button in the header bar or startup screen If your program doesn't use a button, look in the Options or Settings pull-down menu.

○ The screen should look something like Figure 4.2.

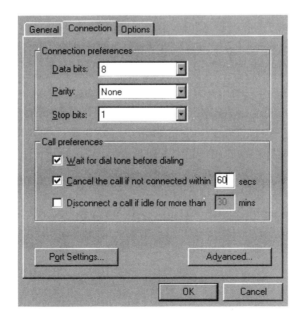

Figure 4.2 *Configuring your modem.*

○ Tab between the fields and enter the appropriate information.

○ Click **OK** or **Save**.

> If you change service providers, physical locations, or contact a different modem, be sure to check your communications parameters. The most common communications error (outside of not having the phone plugged in) is having the wrong parameters. If you are not sure what parameters your office or school or colleague is using simply ask them and then reconfigure your modem but don't forget to switch back when you get back online.

FILE-TRANSFER PROTOCOLS

Unless you are transferring files or exchanging data with other online users, you will seldom have a need to set or change your computer's *File Transfer Protocol (FTP). File transfer protocols* are the language two communicating computers speak regardless of the operating platform or communications software being used. A *protocol* dictates how a file is broken into blocks of data and performs comparisons of each block at both the sending and receiving ends. If these comparisons are valid, the block is sent; if they are not, the block is re-sent. While the most common protocol used is Zmodem the most important thing is that both communicating computers are using the same protocol.

Phone Connection

The final piece to the hardware puzzle is the physical connection to your telephone system. The phone line you use can be your existing voice line, just remember that if you have any extensions, you won't be able to use them for voice calls while you are online.

For first time users we recommend they start by utilizing their existing voice line and if they find their time online necessitates an additional line to add it later. We also suggest to parents that they establish some special times or "online windows" so that your kids can get online. Make sure these special online times don't coincide with a time that Mom or Dad will be trying to call from the office.

Making the actual connection is simple. Virtually every new home built uses modular RJ–11 jacks for phone connections. These are the square plastic connections with a tab to hold them in the socket that attach to the end of your phone line. To connect your modem simply remove the phone line from the wall by pressing down the tab and pulling gently outward. Your modem undoubtedly came with a phone cable that can be used to connect the modem to the wall jack but if you need a longer cable you can obtain one of these at your local hardware or electronics store. Insert one end of this cable into the wall jack and the other into the socket on the modem labeled "line." This socket will look similar to the opening in the wall for your phone.

If you have one of those homes that has older 4-prong jacks, is hardwired (no way to remove a phone without cutting the cord), or is still using rotary phones, you will require some physical changes to your phone wiring. While this is a how-to book, electrical, plumbing, framing, and roofing concerns remain well outside the realm of this authors expertise and are best left to the professionals. A call to your local telephone company will be sufficient to initiate any changes that are required to create a computer connection in your home.

To finish the connection, insert the line from your phone into the socket on the modem labeled "phone" (now your phone will work like it always did except when you are online) and connect the modem to the appropriate port on the back of your computer.

For those who have "extra" features on their phones (call waiting, distinctive ringing, etc.) or live in an area that requires you dial an area code but not dial "1" before the area code these are all things you must keep in mind when making your connections and configuring your modem.

Choosing a Service Provider

Your computer is plugged in, the new phone line is in, and the modem is connected. You have disks from America Online, CompuServe, Prodigy, PipelineUSA, and NETCOM. Each is beckoning you: "Join Us Online," "10 Free Hours," "New Graphical Interface". So you might ask:

- ❍ "Why not get on each one, try my 10 hours and see which one I like?"

- ❍ "All I do is pop their disk into the drive and now I am on the Internet, right?"

- ❍ "How do I decide which one to use?"

These are questions we hear every day from parents, educators, and kids alike. And the answers are: "Go ahead, why not," "Not exactly," and "Read on!"

As I noted in Chapter 2, regardless of how you get there, your online destination ought to be the Internet. Never has this been more true than today. Prices of Internet access continue to drop, while Internet service providers provide even more customer service in an effort to differentiate themselves. More and more of the once proprietary services of commercial service providers are being made available to Internet users in an effort by them to retain their current user base.

Six months ago I would have told you that your choice of an online provider would be determined by the services you want to access, the tools you want to use, the money you want to spend, the degree of user-friendliness you prefer, how much you want to use the Internet, and the amount of time you want to spend online. Today the entire online world is migrating toward the Internet. It seems you can't pick up a newspaper, magazine, or trade publication without being reminded that if you are not on the Internet (and getting your business operating online too) you are behind the times.

As little as a year ago, the introduction of graphical interfaces to the Internet by commercial service providers was being heralded in product reviews. Meanwhile, the commercial services themselves scorned the Internet as a wild and untamed place where unpredictable and "bad" things happened and that the really good stuff could only be found on their services. However, in the last year, the world has ever so quietly changed. No longer is it us versus them, but rather: "Look how easy our service makes it to get to the Internet." Commercial service providers simply found that it didn't make sense to stand there with their finger in the dike while the dike washed down around them.

To Surf or Not to Surf: That's Not the Question Anymore

So much has the world changed in favor of the Internet that you are seeing commercial providers making unprecedented changes. America Online has recently allowed users to begin using Netscape's award-winning browser in addition to their own WebBrowser. CompuServe has gone as far as to migrate onto the Internet by making all of their new product development work correspond with Internet accessible standards.

So the question today really becomes one of cost, followed by what additional services do I need or want and how much am I willing to pay for those services above and beyond the basic Internet access and customer service.

There are five major commercial service providers (CSPs) and an ever growing number of both local and national internet service providers (ISPs) who can accomplish the task of getting you onto the Internet. In this chapter we will review each of the major service providers. We will help you understand both the similarities and the differences between the various providers and where a difference exists, just how that might affect your decision making process. As with any purchase, the informed purchaser gets the most for their money and are usually the happiest with their purchase. This chapter will help you achieve both.

Summary

I know this is an odd place for a summary but I also know that what you really want to know is what service provider you should be using so you can get on with the really important stuff—getting online. Therefore, I have condensed my recommendation to the beginning of this chapter. Following my recommendation is a table that will allow you to compare that recommendation with the other service providers. I will discuss each of those other service providers just in case you decide not to follow my recommendation.

INTERNET SERVICE PROVIDERS: THE ONLY REAL CHOICE

With the commercial service providers migrating towards the Internet, the driving issue for selecting a service provider becomes cost. Dollar for dollar, internet service providers provide better value. Certainly other factors should influence *which* ISP you choose, but if what you want is the Internet at a reasonable rate, with good service, good customer support, and parental controls that are truly effective at keeping your kids from inappropriate materials, an ISP is your only real choice.

Table 5.1 Comparison of common service provider services

		NETCOM	America Online	CompuServe	Microsoft Network	Prodigy
Basic Information	Telephone Number	(800)638-2661	(800) 827-6364	(800) 848-8199	(800) 386-5550	(800) 776-3449
	Number of Subscribers	400,000	> 5 million	2.5 million	800,000	2 million
What It Costs	Base Rate	$19.95	$9.95	$9.95	$9.95	$9.95
	w/ 1 Child	$19.95	$39.45	$39.45	$39.45	$39.45
	w/ 2 Children	$19.95	$68.95	$68.95	$68.95	$68.95
	For 40 hours/month	$19.95	$113.20	$113.20	$113.20	$113.20
	Introductory Offer	$5.00 first month / unlimited hours	First month's fee waived; 10 free hours	First month's fee waived; 10 free hours	First month's waived; 10 free hours	First month's fee waived; 10 free hours
Standard Features	Internet Access	Access to all Internet services	WWW, FTP, Newsgroups Only	WWW, Telnet, FTP, Newsgroups	WWW, Telnet, Newsgroups Only	WWW, FTP, Newsgroups Only
	E-mail	Yes	Yes	Yes	Yes	Yes
	Chat Areas	Yes	Yes	Yes	Yes	Yes
	News	Yes	Yes	Yes	Yes	Yes
	Shopping	Yes	Yes	Yes	Yes	Yes
Additional Features	Parental Controls	Req. 3rd Party	Yes for AOL - Partial for Internet	Yes	No	Yes on service - Cyber Patrol for Internet
	Offline Automation	Automatic Logon, automatic E-mail retrieval, read/write mail. read downloaded newsgroups send/receive mail, Automated access	Automatic Logon, read/write mail send/recieve Flash sessions	Automatic Logon, automatic E-mail and file retrieval read/write mail, read downloaded newsgroups send/receive mail	Using MS Exchange can read/write mail offline, send/ receive mail. Automatic logon	Automatic Logon

Table 5.1 (continued)

	NETCOM	America Online	CompuServe	Microsoft Network	Prodigy
Service & Support					
Connecting Speeds	28.8Kbps	supports up to 28.8 Kbps modems in some areas	supports up to 28.8Kbps modems in some areas w/ some 57.6 ISDN support	supports up to 28.8Kbps modems in larger areas, Mostly 9600 & 14.4Kbps	supports up to 28.8Kbps modems in some areas
Online Help	Via E-mail	Bulletin Board & live technicians	Bulletin Board	text-based Help menu	Bulletin Board
Phone Support	(408) 983-5970	(800) 827-3338	(800) 848-8199	(800) 386-5550	(800) 776-3449
International Access	Yes surcharges apply	Several countries; surcharges apply	150 countries; surcharges apply	Dozens of countries; surcharges apply	Canada
Versions Available	DOS, Windows, Mac	DOS, Windows, Mac	DOS, Windows, Mac, O/S2	Windows95 Only	DOS, Windows, Mac
Best Suited For:	Every one	Home Users	Businesses and professionals	Home users	Families w/Kids

Why an Internet Service Provider

Though both ISP and commercial providers are commercial entities, they play significantly different roles. Recall from Chapter 3 that commercial providers developed when you and I did not have access to the Internet. As such, they not only had to introduce people to a whole new way of communicating, but because they could not access the data on the Internet, commercial service provider's also had to develop the content for those services. Therein lies the difference. Commercial providers spend huge sums on developing proprietary content, much of which already exist in some form on the Internet. In order to recoup those costs, they charge fees that range from two to three times what you will pay for access to the Internet directly.

Conversely, the cost and subsequent fees to use ISPs are quite low because they are information carriers. ISPs provide the infrastructure that allows their subscribers to connect to the Internet and to the data that resides there. But they play no role in the data's development. They leave that to the experts—individual users or corporations, libraries, universities who research, create, publish, and ultimately distribute their information to the world via the Internet. ISPs have no more a role in developing the content on the Internet than the phone company does in the conversation you have with your mom and dad on Sunday nights. With the advent of open access to the Internet in 1988, it was inevitable that a differentiation between creators and providers would arise. Commercial service providers were never "experts" in the subject areas anyway. They either paid, or were paid by, third parties to develop material for what was then a captive audience who would pay monthly fees for the information.

Just as important as the *why* is the *why not*. There are a great many myths about ISPs that quite frankly weren't always myths. Let me address a few of the most common ones to put you at ease.

○ **ISPs are not as easy to use.** Early attempts by ISPs at creating an integrated software product to access the Internet were sloppy at best. However today's "front-ends" as they are called, are every bit as user-friendly as the best of the commercial providers.

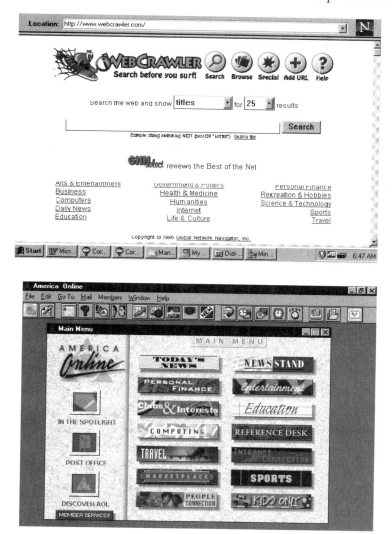

Figure 5.1 Internet or commercial service provider. Either will get you where you want to go.

Figure 5.1 puts NETCOM's (a national ISP) front end side-by-side with AOL's. You can see that both will take you easily to a vast array of sources at the click of the mouse. However with NETCOM, if you wish to access another part of the Internet, say email, you simply click on the email icon and without quitting the Web, you can compose and send your email. I will simply let the numbers speak for themselves. In fifteen years the commercial providers combined have accumulated approximately 8 million users. On the other hand, in 7 years the Internet has accumulated approximately 35 million users. I can understand how a few might be wrong but would 4 times the number of users all make it harder on themselves?

◯ **It is hard to find what you are looking for on the Internet.** Anyone who is making that claim clearly hasn't used the search engines that have been developed to help Internet users do exactly that—find what they are looking for. Yahoo, Webcrawler, and Lycos, among others (see our home page in Appendix B) have made finding what you want as easy as typing in the topic and hitting **Return.** Within seconds, sites from around the world with information about your topic are just a mouse click away. I do wonder though, if it were all that hard to find things on the Internet why would virtually every commercial provider be creating ways for you to access the Internet?

◯ **ISPs can't provide support you like the big companies can.** The fact is that many of the ISPs are big companies themselves though no single ISP supports as may users as the largest commercial provider does. Some of last year's biggest initial public stock offerings were both national and local ISPs and while those offerings created some very wealthy individuals, it also gave those companies a great deal of operating capital to create technical support groups and phone banks all aimed at one thing—increased support and quality. Why? The answer is simple. In the face of continually dropping prices (no they haven't hit the bottom yet) support and quality are one of the few ways to differentiate your service. I have never once been unable to get a technician on the line at NETCOM — 24 hours a day, 7 days a week. I can't remember the last time I was able to actually get through to a CompuServe technical service representative.

○ **The quality of service isn't as good.** One of the distinct advantages the ISPs do have in being recent entrants to the field, is that very little of their equipment is obsolete. Much of that equipment has been purchased during the last five years and takes advantage of the numerous developments that have taken place in communications technology. The result as you might expect is better service, not worse. In the two years I have been using virtually all of the services, I have consistently received faster connections, more often, with fewer dropped lines by using ISPs, than with any of the commercial providers. But I don't expect you to believe me. Try it out for yourself.

SELECTING AN ISP

Selecting an ISP is certainly more difficult than just taking the disk that came in the mail and popping it in the disk drive. Just remember that not all ISPs are created equal so when you are selecting one be careful. "Careful of what?" you might ask. Well get a piece of paper and read on. If you will make a list of these items and keep it in front of you when you call prospective providers you will have a much greater chance of success.

○ **Is the connection a PPP or SLIP connection?** If not, thank them and hang up. I won't go into the technical reasons here but the only type of connection you want is a PPP or SLIP connection to the Internet.

○ **How much does it cost?** Many companies are still offering base rate plus hourly fee arrangements. These may look attractive but a flat rate alleviates so many problems. Keep calling until you find a flat rate between $15 to $20 a month for unlimited usage.

○ **How does the software operate and can you try it out or see it in operation?** You are looking for two basic things here: 1) The package is an integrated solution—it provides software to access all of the major Internet services (WWW, IRC, email, Newsgroups, Telnet, and Gopher) in a single, icon-driven package. 2) The package is self-loading—the extent of your setup role is putting the disk(s) in the drive and filling out a couple of forms on the computer screen.

○ **What modem speeds do they support in your area?** Look for a provider that supports 28.8Kbps modems as an absolute minimum. As I mentioned earlier, the speed of your modem is more important than the speed of your computer. Don't get caught short with a provider who isn't investing in newer, faster technology. Do make sure that the modems they support in your area are 28.8Kbps. Having a 28.8 modem won't do you much good if your ISP doesn't support it.

○ **Do they have customer service reps available online (email) as well as via phone?** Ask what the average telephone wait time for customer service is. If the sales person doesn't know ask to speak to the customer service manager. What you are looking for is some assurance that you won't be on the phone for three days before you get to talk to someone. It is also nice to be able to send an email message to solve a problem, so make sure they have this capability.

○ **Do they make third-party parental controls available and at what cost?** This is probably the least of your worries. These products are easily available once you get online but it never hurts to ask. Many providers offer a package free of charge. So you don't have any unpleasant surprises, make sure you read Chapter 8 before you decide to rely on the package that came with your service.

ISPS AND PARENTAL CONTROLS

Chapter 8 is devoted entirely to those products that are designed to offer parents control over the types of material available to their children online. I won't comment here other than to say that these programs are very effective in blocking out material *you* find offensive without having someone else impose their moral standard on your family. One product in particular, CyberPatrol, is so effective that several of the commercial providers have adopted it as their mode of parental control for their Internet gateway. With regards to parental controls, one of the distinct advantages of selecting an ISP is there are no cracks between the services for controls to fall into. For instance, Prodigy provides controls for the chat groups and forums on its service but when you go to the Internet, CyberPatrol must take over and limit access. With only one service, there is no transfer of control. Only one product is responsible for maintaining the integrity of your parental control filters. It is important to point out that no scheme for control on any service will be fool proof, but these access control products are very, very good.

Getting Started

The specifics on getting started will lie with the service provider you choose, but in general it should be as easy to get your Internet connection up and running as it is to install a new piece of software. This task will be greatly simplified if you are using Windows 95 or a Macintosh. But even in Windows 3.1 it should be little more than typing **a:install** and filling out a couple of forms on the screen with information about you and your billing method.

The startup screen will also vary but should look something like that shown in Figure 5.2 with icons to click on to get to the various services of the Internet. The exercises in Chapter 7 will help you get started once you have logged on.

Commercial Service Providers

Several years ago there were a number of commercial service providers from which to choose. Today only four remain. A brief overview of each is provided below.

America Online (AOL)

As one of the most popular and easy-to-use commercial providers, AOL reminds me of the kid's joke about the three hundred pound gorilla. Where does he sleep? Anywhere he wants to. The friendly "Welcome" and "You Have Mail" of AOLs easy-to-use interface mask the power behind the animal. Since its launch in 1989, AOL has accumulated nearly five million users and while accurate user numbers are hard to get, AOL is likely the largest and fastest growing online service provider. This is due in no small part to an aggressive marketing campaign that aims at putting free startup software into the hands of millions of people through direct mailings and magazines. Even a recent Sunday paper had a free diskette sealed into the plastic wrapper. If you haven't received one of these disks yet, just ask a neighbor, they probably have six or seven, or give AOL a call.

America Online
8619 Westwood Center Drive
Vienna, VA 22182
(800) 827-6364 or (703) 448-8700
Costs: $9.95/month (includes 5 hours online)
$2.95 each additional hour

Figure 5.2 Startup screen from NETCOM , a national ISP, with Webcrawler as the default home page.

Overview

The sheer size of AOL has allowed them to do things no other provider can. The large consumer market AOL users represent has attracted more advertisers, more online magazines, more educational activities—more, more, more. A look at the startup screen (see Figure 5.3) lets you know that there is something for everybody. A news area lets you catch up on the day's headlines. There is a section to help you with your finances and keep up with the markets. There are also online magazines, a reference area, games and other activities, chat rooms, online shopping, and sports updates. KOOL (Kids Only Online) is a place strictly for kids.

Figure 5.3 From AOLs startup screen the possibilities are endless.

And that is just the tip of the iceberg. Under the **GoTo** menu, select **Keywords** and you can instantly go to dozens of places reflected by the names shown. In the extensive use I have made of AOL, I have yet to find a topic on which there wasn't some information. However, this points up several of AOL's greatest weaknesses; the depth of information available and getting to it. The depth of information on a particular topic often leaves me wanting more. This is understandable given the number of interests a single source is attempting to satisfy, but all the same, to satisfy my needs, a provider must offer greater depth of information from more sources. In general I also find the information cumbersome to get to but not all that bad given the number of topics being presented.

AOL and the Internet

AOL recently announced that their users can use the highly regarded Netscape® browser instead of or in addition to AOL's proprietary browser. AOL users will also be able to use Microsoft's Internet Explorer. These changes will greatly enhance their service and will do a great deal to overcome the depth of information concern. I still find it amazing that the commercial provider's haven't found a way to seamlessly integrate the Internet's functions into their own (see the Prodigy discussion that follows). However, the use of competing browsers is at least a step in the right direction.

AOL also restricts Internet access to the World Wide Web, Usenet Newsgroups, email, and Gopher searches. This eliminates a great deal of material available on the Internet that would only be available by adding an additional ISP provider.

One final item about AOL and the Internet is access. See the following section "Bumps In The Road" for more detail, but suffice it to say that getting to the Internet with any reliability on AOL is nearly impossible.

Getting Started with AOL

If your computer didn't already come pre-loaded with a copy of AOL, you will need a copy of their software. These can be purchased bundled with other "helpful" references, etc. but I would ask around and see if someone you know hasn't already received a copy in the mail that they will give you.

For Windows, begin by inserting the disk in the A: drive. From the Windows Program Manager File menu select **Run** and type **a:setup** (on a Macintosh double-click the disk icon and drag the program file to your desktop or hard drive). The entire start-up process will take about ten minutes. Make sure you have the materials that came with the disk handy as these will have the password to use that will enable your free hours. You will also need a credit card or checking account number for future billing purposes. You will be asked to select a screen name and a password that will be yours and yours alone online.

Warning

Two words of caution here: 1) Choose your screen name carefully as it cannot be changed without closing your account and establishing another. Many times people have chosen these names flippantly to find out later they cannot be changed. 2) Remember your password. No one will ever ask you for your password from AOL and they cannot (or will not) look it up for you.

If your modem is installed, turned on, and connected properly, you will here AOL dial a special 800 number and ask you for your local area code. Based on your input it will return the local AOL number for your area that your modem will call from now on. AOL has local phone numbers for virtually every major metropolitan area and most rural ones as well, but if for some reason you area doesn't have one, you will have to decide whether to incur the additional surcharge to use AOL's 800 number on an ongoing basis (this would be just like making a long distance call every time you went online) or using a different service with a local connection. Once you have selected a phone number the modem will disconnect and dial again using your newly selected number.

Once online you will see the startup screen (Figure 5.3) but in front of it you will see the box titled America Online Update. During your first time online and virtually every time thereafter, when you log on this box will come up to tell you AOL is adding new art to your files (see the following section on Cons). From here on out the sky is the limit. Try out everything. Click on the **icon** next to the New icon in your menu bar to go onto the Internet and check it out. If you are worried about how long you have been online, the clock icon in the top corner will tell you how long you have been online for the current session.

Should you need help once you are online Member Services is the place to start. From the **Members** menu select **Members Services.** When you enter this area the clock keeping track of the amount of billable time stops running and any time you spend solving a problem or helping others in the Members Services area is free. Once you leave Member Services the clock will start running again. The Tech Live Center and E-mail to Staff areas are great places to get help from the experts if you have problems or questions. Or you might try the Members Helping Members area to get help from the real experts, the AOL community of users.

Parental Controls

AOL was one of the first commercial providers to introduce a series of controls parents can implement to ostensibly filter out material inappropriate for children. I say ostensibly because my experiences with filters have shown the claims to be far better than the results. To activate the Parental Controls feature simply go the **Members** menu and select **Parental Controls.** AOL allows you to exercise controls over three areas: 1) chat groups, 2) downloading of files, and 3) newsgroups. From this screen you can change the controls exercised for each user in your family for each of these areas or you can choose to limit access for all users to the Kids Only area.

AOLs parental controls focus mainly on restricting the proprietary services AOL offers. However, the Newsgroup control area does allow parents to block access to Internet newsgroups. In this area, parents can choose to either block no newsgroups, all newsgroups, allow access to groups they have previously previewed and entered into the control panel, or block access to groups whose names contain words or letter groupings of a parent's choosing. In this way newsgroups whose names contain "sex," "porno," "pictures," "uck," gasm," etc. or any other desired selections.

In addition to the parental controls section, AOL does several other things which I believe lead to the creation of a constructive environment for online usage.

1. The ability to create multiple names on one account and set limits for each of those names, allows parents to move from a one-size-fits-all arena to creating an appropriate environment for each child based on their age, maturity level, interests and propensity for abiding by "the rules."

2. AOL states their rules of conduct up front, and provides online monitoring to supervise posting and activities. These monitoring activities are most effective in the Kid Only section but are by no means 100% effective.

It is important to note that the parental controls on AOL lack the ability to regulate activity in several areas that I think are important:

○ **Access to the World Wide Web (via the Internet gateway).** I am fond of telling parents who doubt the presence of inappropriate material on the Web that if they will give me five minutes they will leave in three. I firmly believe that if I can find it in three minutes your teens can find it in less than that.

○ **Access to the Internet altogether.** In the absence of any controls over areas such as the WWW, some sort of control should be available to disable Internet access, without it being an all or nothing decision.

○ **Limitations based on words or letter groupings for the actual content of chat rooms.** Situations and language that would make the crustiest of sailors blush occur in chat rooms and newsgroups whose titles have nothing to do with inappropriate topics all the time. I was personally embarrassed last Valentines

Day when I curiously stepped into the chat room called "Heart to Heart." Trust me when I tell you it was anything but hearts they were discussing there.

Bumps in the Road

Several things should color your decision to become a member of the America Online community.

The graphical nature of AOL is one of its strongest features but the intensity of these graphics can frustrate even the most patient consumer. If your modem is anything less than a 14.4Kbps, consider either a different service, a new modem or at the very least, turning off some of the graphical features in the Preferences area online. An annoyance you can't avoid will be "update downloads" that happen virtually every time you log on. All of the graphics for every department don't come on the single disk AOL sent you. Therefore, the first time you log on to a particular area, AOL must download whatever graphics are associated with that area. Depending on the speed of your modem and that of your local connection, this can take seconds or an annoyingly long period of minutes. None of this would be particularly annoying if it weren't for the fact that the entire time these files are downloading, the clock is ticking making the "blue Thermometer" an unwelcome friend.

Warning　The other screens you will come to loath are the commercial advertisements that appear when you sign on (see Figure 5.4). Each time you sign on AOL presents, for you to either Order or Cancel, a product they are promoting. I am sure that most of these products are useful and that many of AOL's customers gladly purchase them. However, I have heard one too many stories of inadvertent ordering and been delayed one too many times from getting quickly to the subject at hand to accept these ads as a benefit.

WHAT ARE ALL THESE BOOKS?

A recent seminar participant shared his story about these "Order Screens" on AOL. His son is eight and frequented the KOOL areas of AOL. In many windows applications, after selecting a particular action you click on **OK**. When unsolicited books and computer products began showing up from America Online, a few questions revealed that this man's son thought he had to click that button to log on to AOL. He had simply mistaken OK for Order.

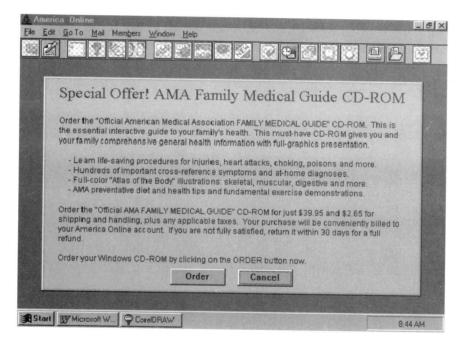

Figure 5.4 *Want to order? Don't click the wrong button.*

Despite the good intentions AOL has in implementing its parental controls, they remain highly ineffective for anything but the most inexperienced user. In fact, when I am looking for a particularly steamy online conversation to demonstrate for parents, it is often one of many innocuously named chat rooms on AOL where I will go.

If the Internet is indeed your destination, the combination of local connection speeds and the number of users trying to connect at a given time can create intolerable delays. At anything but the wee hours of the morning on the east coast, accessing the Internet on AOL is something of a challenge. If you can get a connection at all, the delays in transferring data and downloading graphics will squelch even the most patient persons desire to "go surfing."

The final issue is one of cost. At the time of this printing, AOL was proposing new cost structures that would allow users to be online for 20 hours for $20, with additional hours costing $2.95. Take our model of kids using the computer as much as they watch TV and you will see that with two kids you could easily spend 40 hours per month online. To accentuate the matter simply add your own usage into that calculation and you could easily spend $50 to $100 per month for AOL access. Compare this to a flat rate of $20 per month for unlimited access and you will understand why I recommend parents strongly consider their choices before making a decision on an access provider.

COMPUSERVE

If AOL is the gorilla in the jungle, CompuServe would have to be the wise old owl. Launched in 1969, CompuServe is the oldest of the online services. CompuServe began when a Columbus, Ohio insurance company began renting mainframe computer time to area businesses. Today it is owned by H&R Block and has grown to approximately 3.5 million users. Given this maturity, it is not surprising that CompuServe began with a strong business and professional orientation. After all, in 1970 personal computers weren't really personal and only businesses could afford to use them. Though greatly expanded, that orientation remains even today with CompuServe's major focus being on financial information, news, reference material, and computer hardware and software support through its personal computing forums.

CompuServe

5000 Arlington Center Boulevard

Columbus, OH 43220

(800) 849-8199 or (614) 529-1349

Costs: $9.95/month (includes 5 hours online)

$2.95 each additional hour

Overview

CompuServe is no place for the novice user. Its major service categories include News/Weather, Sports, Magazines, Computers, Home & Leisure, Entertainment, Education, Professional Services, Financial Information, Shopping and the Internet just like any of the other services but from the moment you log on you know it is different. Perhaps it is the logon procedure or the look of the initial screen but somehow it is just more computer.

CompuServe's strong suit is its vast array of information. Where AOL lacked depth, CompuServe makes up for it ten times over. More than 3000 databases, 50,000 journals, more than 100 online publications, huge libraries of shareware and public domain software programs, live discussion groups, and special interest forums, continuous stock updates and analysis combine to make CompuServe one of the largest data sources outside the Internet. Of course, if what you want still isn't here, you can connect to the Internet through CompuServe's gateway and find it there.

Having the information is one thing, but getting to it is really the heart of the matter and here is where CompuServe excels. Like AOL, CompuServe uses a "GO Word" system of getting you quickly from place to place. Once you know the Go word for a particular area, you simply choose **Go** from the **Services** menu, type that word in and you are there. But the real gems are the search capabilities and navigation option. This is particularly true for so vast an information base as it would be easy to get lost in the data without these tools. By simply selecting **Topics of Interest** from the **Services** menu, you can find your way to the most minute topic. The navigation option uses your computer to retrieve the information and let you read it later offline, and with CompuServe's rates, this is probably a good thing.

Despite recent changes in pricing policies, I still feel nickeled-and-dimed when I use CompuServe. Where the Internet is a flat fee for all access and AOL has a base plus hourly arrangement, CompuServe takes that and adds additional fees for participating in certain forums, or for using a higher speed modem (if CompuServe can't get it in time online, they will get it in surcharges), accessing and searching some databases and downloading articles. The good news is that at least they have dropped their fees for email. With the new pricing structure email is now billed at the hourly connect time rate rather than a per message rate.

Note   One last note of caution about cost. When canceling your service, do so well in advance of the last day of the month. CompuServe bills on the last Saturday of the month so if you wait until the last day of the month, most times you will have been billed for the next month even though you will have canceled several days after you were billed. Not that CompuServe won't reverse the charges, it is just something you don't want to hassle with.

For all its good intentions, CompuServe just has poor manners. Despite a more graphical interface and its robust search and retrieve tools, CompuServe remains a service geared toward the serious computer user with online experience. Most users simply won't take advantage of all the material available and the presence of so much material makes getting lost that much easier. Coupled with this is a sign-up procedure that even frustrated me, impersonal and erratic customer service, and a "traditional computer" feel, making CompuServe a disaster for novice online users. Certainly not a place for kids, the timid, or the shy. Perhaps CompuServe's new WOW Service will better suit these users needs. It is only planned for Windows 95 users so I won't hold my breath.

CompuServe and the Internet

CompuServe provides a gateway to the Internet that includes its own World Wide Web browser, access to FTP and IRC sites as well as access to Usenet Newsgroups and Gopher sites. While none of these are exceptionally cumbersome to use, neither are they as good as either Netscape or NetCruiser. That said, the recent announcement by CompuServe that all future development work will be done in accordance with HTML standards (read that as Internet ready) and that more of their previously proprietary services will become available to Internet users will bring CompuServe closer to looking like an ISP than any of the other commercial providers.

Getting Started

Installation for novice users can be summed up in three words—Don't do it! If however, you can't resist the temptation that free diskettes and 10 hours online provides, here goes. CompuServe can be accessed from either a standard communications package or using the CompuServe Information Manager (CIM) for either Windows, DOS or Macintosh systems. If you do not want to use the CIM software, call (800) 848-8990 and request a local access number, a user ID, and a password. However, I would suggest using the CIM as it makes CompuServe easier to use.

Begin the installation by inserting CIM Disk 1 into the A: drive. Select **Run** from the **File** menu and enter **a:setup** and click **OK**. Follow the onscreen prompts (as best you can) installing Disk 2 when prompted to do so. Make sure that you have the documentation that came with your disks as well as a credit card handy. You will need the agreement number and serial number from them to complete the login process. Respond **Yes** when asked if you want to sign up as part of the installation process and CompuServe will fill out most of the required information for you. You can (and should) even select Autodetect at the modem selection prompt and let the computer do the work for you. Finally, you will need to answer a few more questions and CompuServe will you with a temporary User ID and password. Write these down and keep them safe until you receive the real one several weeks later. Why is it that every other service I have dealt with can handle this task online and CompuServe must do this via the mail is beyond me but that the way it is done, for now.

Note

One last point on installation. Though CompuServe supports a number of 28.8 and 57.6Kbps modems, you will be installed at 2400. Be sure to change this by clicking on **Special, Session Settings** once you are online.

Once you have completed the setup procedures, start WinCIM by double clicking **WinCIM** in the CompuServe folder in your Program Manager (or the Hard Drive icon for you Macintosh users). With Windows 95, click **Start**, click **Programs**, click **CompuServe** and click **CompuServe Information Manager**. Then click **Connect** and you are online. Safe Surfing!

Parental Controls

CompuServe recently began offering parental controls to those concerned about their kids access to inappropriate materials. online. To access these controls use the **Go** menu and select **Controls**. CompuServe controls restrict access to those Internet services accessible through CompuServe —Newsgroups, file transfer protocol, and Telnet—as we;; as certain areas on the CompuServe Information Service.

CompuServe also allows control of direct Internet access through the use of third-party software—CyberPatrol. Click on the red Internet Controls button to download this software and put road blocks between your kids and adult-only material.

Bumps in the Road

CompuServe's niche in the market has never been the novice user and it remains so today. That does not make CompuServe a bad service provider. Note the 3.5 million users and you will see that it has a loyal cadre of users who make use of the extensive information available. It just isn't the service of choice for parents who are new to the online world and are looking to create a fun, inviting and user-friendly environment for themselves as well as their kids.

CompuServe suffers from the same antiquated pricing structure as AOL with the additional burden of surcharges for "special" areas.

I found the process of initiating service extremely cumbersome. From the beginning the process asks questions the novice user would have no idea how to answer. Service names and passwords aren't something you choose but instead they are assigned though you can change them in a couple of weeks when your new password is mailed to you. Selecting local service numbers is supposedly done for you but no local numbers were available for as large a metropolitan area as Atlanta!?! All in all the process was just more than a person who is still trying to figure out what the red button on the side of the computer is for should have to endure.

PRODIGY

Of all the commercial providers, Prodigy gets my vote for the casual user looking for an excellent starting place for getting introduced to online services. It is by far and away the easiest to install, the new Internet connections make more information available and make it much easier to get to; and there are a variety of children's topics and parental controls that are not the greatest but will do until you switch to an ISP.

The Prodigy Service
445 Hamilton Avenue
White Plains, NY 10601
(800) 776-0845 or (800) 776-3449
Costs: $9.95/month (includes 5 hours online)
$2.95 each additional hour
30/30 Plan provides 30 hours access for $29.95
w/ each additional hour over 30 at $2.95

Overview

Prodigy's real strength is its focus on the family. What CompuServe is to the business and professional user, Prodigy is to families with kids. It is easy to use and understand and provides a variety of software and activities for parents and children alike. If you have used Prodigy in the past, try the new version. It is colorful and packed with graphics to illustrate children's interactive stories and games, not to mention the graphics associated with the Internet's World Wide Web. One of our kids' favorites is Sesame Street. Prodigy has the same major areas as the other providers, News & Weather, Business/Finance, Sports, Entertainment, Shopping, Computing, Travel, the Internet, Kids Zone and one of my favorites, Teen Turf. Moving between these areas is accomplished with either icons and buttons or "Jump" words similar to the keyword system used by AOL and the Go words used in CompuServe. Online help is plentiful with onscreen instructions to assist you as you move through a particular process and when you are expected to do something—the button you are supposed to click will blink.

Prodigy would also have to win the prize when it comes to online advertising. This has both an up- and downside. For those disillusioned purists who believe the Internet should operate without commercial promotion, the very presence alone of commercial promotion will make your blood boil. However, for the rest of us who from time to time are interested in shopping online, Prodigy's method of company icons being the only promotion on the screen is a real plus over the full-page advertisements of AOL. If a particular company's icon interests you, click on it and a full-screen ad will appear or you may even be transported to the Internet to view their World Wide Web site.

Several areas are tailored for younger users. Kids Zone and Teen Turf allow your kids to access educational games, reference materials (online journals, encyclopedias, etc.) , entertainment, Web sites for kids and special chat areas just for them. One last place of special interest to the kids will be the Homework Helper in the More About Kids Zone option. Kids ask the service a question and tell it the resources they want to use and it searches 1,500 books, 500 magazines, 100 newspapers, 1,500 photos and 300 maps to find a number of items they can download.

Prodigy and the Internet

Bravo! A seamless interface to the Internet from a commercial service provider. Could it be? Yes, Prodigy has accomplished what all of the biggest players combined could not do. One of Prodigy's strongest attributes is their Internet browser that makes the Internet as close as a point and click. This onramp takes you instantly from the links built into Prodigy's various categories of interest to Web sites without the use of the cumbersome gateway that others use. You can even use the Personal Web Page feature to create your own site on the Internet that others can visit without any special programming knowledge. But most importantly, if you are unfamiliar with the Internet, you will find numerous resources to get you surfing.

Getting Started

Of all the services we tested, Prodigy was by far and away the easiest to install. Yes, even easier than the Microsoft Network. Prodigy is often preloaded on new computers but if yours did not come with a copy simply call the Prodigy Services Company to get the software directly or you can purchase a start up kit through your local computer store.

The handbook that comes with the software does a great job of introducing the service and taking you through the start-up process. To get started in Windows insert the disk into the **a: drive.** Select **Run** from the **File** menu and enter **A:setup** and click **OK** and follow the onscreen prompts. The whole process will take ten minutes or less and most of that your hands are nowhere near the keyboard. The software searches for the modem, fills in the needed information, and creates a program group in Windows. About the only thing you will have to do is answer a series of billing questions the first time you log on and tell the computer your area code so that it can find a local access number. Another plus is the automatic update of the software if you are using an older version. These updates are done free of charge and you are prompted so you know what is happening and how long it will take. Versions are available for Windows, DOS, and Macintosh.

You will be asked to enter your **User ID** and **password** but even this can be automated if you so desire. From the **Go To** menu select **Tools** and click **Autologon**. Once online, you will see the Highlights screen which is your window to the Prodigy service. Simply click on any of the major categories on the right side of the screen, select one of the special features on the left or select from the pull-down menus. If you don't see something that strikes your fancy, click **Interest Groups A-Z** in the services menu on the right side of the Highlights screen and type in your subject. As you discover places of interest, add them to your "hot list" so you can easily come back to them. From the particular site you like simply click the **Go To** menu and select **Add to Hot List.** Now to get back to that particular site all you will have to do is click the **Hot List** tab at the bottom of the screen and click on the site you want from the list you have created.

Parental Controls

Prodigy has done a great job of creating a number of tools for creating a CyberSafe environment. Not all of these tools are billed as parental control mechanisms but they lead kids to material that is educational, informative, and fun while at the same time allowing parents to manage what material is available to their kids.

One of these tools is the ability to create separate User ID's for each member of your family (up to six). Each ID has a separate password and can be configured to access different parts of the network. Which chat groups, newsgroups, areas of interest, etc. the user can access can all be modified for each individual ID. You can also suspend a particular ID's use privileges which gives parents a great way enforce "the rules." To create or manage User ID's use the **Go To** menu and select **Tools.** Then click **Create/Manage IDs** and follow the directions. Note that the account holder's ID ends in an "A" and that subsequent IDs on the same account will use the same ID number but will end with the letters B–F. From the same screen where you create IDs you can then manage access by User ID.

Another extremely valuable tool for guiding kids to "the good stuff" is the ability to create what Prodigy calls Personal Paths. For each User ID you can customize the Highlights screen and create individual Hot Lists that reflect that user's interests. Just as the tabs on the your Highlight screen might be Finance and News, your child's could be Sports, Entertainment and Games.

From the **Manage Access** area parents can limit a child's access to a number of areas:

○ Chats

○ Instant Messaging

○ Newsgroups

○ Pseudonyms

○ World Wide Web

○ Multiplayer Games

○ email

Once again, click the **Go To** menu and select **Tools.** click **Manage Access** and you will see a screen where you can select the level of access for each User ID by category. Note that for Internet chat (IRC), Newsgroups, and the World Wide Web you can only turn access on or off.

To overcome this shortcoming, Prodigy has partnered with Microsystems, Inc. to offer CyberPatrol, a Internet access control software that will allow parents to selectively manage access to the Internet services available on Prodigy. Cyber Patrol will not manage the Prodigy areas but when you take advantage of Prodigy's link to the Internet it will automatically engage and serve as a filter for those services. CyberPatrol is consistently rated at the top of the list for access control software and best of all is free to Prodigy users. This package not only offers a rich value but also a control solution that we think is the best in the market (See the review of CyberPatrol in Chapter 8).

To load CyberPatrol to your computer, you guessed it, click **Go To**, select **Jump** and type **CyberPatrol** into the box. Click **Jump** and you will be taken to a access screen about CyberPatrol. One of your options there will be to download the software. Click that button and follow the directions for setup. It will take about 15 minutes to download the software (at 9600 baud) but that is a small investment for so powerful a tool. It is worth noting that CyberPatrol is not unique to Prodigy and can be combined with virtually any Internet service to create the same kind of shield from inappropriate material. However, Prodigy is one of the first commercial providers to adopt an outside vendor's product to offer this type of protection.

Bumps in the Road

For all its great features Prodigy does have some shortcomings. The foremost of these is Prodigy's lack of support for high speed modems. The result can be agonizingly slow downloads of graphics, especially if you are used to speedy responses from other providers.

Prodigy's new graphical interface and improved graphics are a welcome change but they are still weak in comparison. Email is downloaded in a large and hard to read font, onscreen buttons while functional are sloppy looking. While none of this makes it easier to use, enhancements would certainly make it easier to look at.

One drawback to Prodigy's CyberPatrol connection is that it will not block access to IRC groups and Newsgroups in Windows 95. Additionally, it cannot be configured for individual users yet, though Microsystems assures us this will be an upcoming change.

MICROSOFT NETWORK (MSN)

Microsoft Network is the new kid on the block today but they very likely may be the bully on the block tomorrow.

Microsoft Inc.
(800) 386-5550
Costs: $4.95/month (includes 3 hours online)
$2.95 each additional hour
or 20/20 plan provides 20 hours for $19.95
w/ each additional hour at $2.00

Overview

With the release of Windows 95 there was a new game in town when it came to online services. Wanting to capitalize on the release of its new operating system, Microsoft bundled Microsoft Network with Windows 95 and presto, instant market penetration. The kind of penetration AOL and others had spent years and millions of dollars to achieve. But one piece is still missing, value. For all the hype in the media and all the fears expressed by commercial providers and in court documents, you would think Microsoft had created the answer to everyone's online prayers. One look around the service and you will wonder like I did what the stink is all about. Sure MSN is easy to get signed onto, but it is not as easy as Prodigy; and Prodigy doesn't come preloaded. It is nowhere near as easy to navigate as AOL nor does it have the breadth of services. And although MSN is supposed to be intuitively easy and just like maneuvering in the Windows environment, I found it anything but easy. Maybe I am just used to online services that make it easy to find what I am looking for without knowing where to look, or maybe Microsoft is betting that the millions of people who have never been online when they receive their new computer will blindly get on MSN and not know to look any further. To AOL, CompuServe, Prodigy and every ISP around the world, keep sending the free disks guys, it ain't over yet!

MSN and the Internet

Like everything else about MSN, once you get there, it's great, but getting there was such a nightmare it wasn't worth it. MSN does not have the capability to search for a specific name or phrase so finding a particular newsgroup, even if you know the name, becomes a bit like going through a room full of unlabeled filing cabinets looking for the file drawer that has the information you are looking for in it. Getting on to the World Wide Web requires a right-mouse click on the little **MSN** icon in the lower right corner of the taskbar, a left-mouse click on **MSN Central,** a click on Categories, a click on **The Internet Center** folder, and a click on the **WWW** icon. Whatever happened to a simple Internet icon that takes you directly to the Internet or better yet, the integration of Internet information into the existing MSN folders with their various topics?

Getting Started

While signing up with MSN was not an exercise in frustration, neither was it a "set it and forget it" routine like Prodigy's either. The first trouble I encountered was I had not loaded MSN's software when I had loaded Windows 95 which meant I had to find the CD-ROM and insert it into the drive. Once that was done, installation was fairly simple. I just had to follow the instructions on the screen, filling in my telephone number, name and address and billing information. Click **Join Now** and up comes the phone number screen again but this time with a local access number and the first surprise I encountered with MSN. In as big a city as Atlanta the fastest modem they support is 9600 bps. (For a company that is shipping pre-loaded software that supports 9600 bps and 14.4Kbps on computers that are for the most part shipping with 14.4Kbps and 28.8Kbps modems seems a little odd.) Click on **OK** and the modem will ask you to choose a screen name and password and that's it, you're on MSN. The first screen you will see is MSN Today and hopefully you are lucky enough to find what you are looking for on that screen. However, if you aren't you will have to go looking. The place to start is MSN Central. Minimize or close the **MSN Today** screen and MSN Central will be hiding behind it. Click **Categories** and the next screen will have a series of folders with vague topical names on them. Here is where the hunt and peck starts. Even using Windows 95's Explore function I was still unable to find any of the topics I went in search of without opening dozens of files and doing lots of unnecessary searching. The long and short of it is this. For less money I can get more, faster and easier using any other service. Until MSN overcomes those shortcomings it will never make it past my desktop.

Parental Controls

MSN does not provide any parental controls as part of their service. There are some restrictions on adult chat areas and newsgroups but to overcome these only requires the user to state that they are over 18 and know that they are participating in adult activities. These could hardly be considered controls when any fourteen-year-old boy can state he is 18 or older and have access to these areas. Imagine if all our teens had to do to buy alcohol was to state they are 21 years old.

Bumps in the Road

If you have wondered why I haven't talked about DOS or Macintosh versions, it is simple, they don't exist. MSN will only work with Windows 95 which makes it clear Microsoft is betting on people stepping up to technology rather than making do with what they have.

I alluded to MSN's second failing in my introduction. It simply isn't easy to find the information you are looking for unless you already know where to look. This struck me as a little like the chicken and the egg and for something as ubiquitous as the Internet extremely shortsighted.

Finally, even though the graphics are great, at the slower modem speeds MSN supports, it just takes too long to download. I was connected at 9600 baud and you could watch the resolution of pictures increase with each pass of the data scan. I hate to think what it would have been like had I been connected on one of those 2400bps lines MSN supports. I am sure that given time Microsoft will work these bugs out but it seems to me that all this may be a little futile with virtually every existing commercial provider going the way of the Internet followed closely by the big three long distance carriers and cable companies.

Setting the Ground Rules

Parents hear so much about the Internet. Television, magazines, and news-papers run sensational stories of problems encountered online. It would be easy for those who are not familiar with the Internet to believe it is a place fraught with danger with little or no redeeming value. However, according to Lawrence J. Magid writing for the National Center for Missing and Exploited Children in *Child Safety on the Information Superhighway* (1994):

○ Although there have been some highly publicized cases of abuse involving computers, reported cases are relatively infrequent.

○ There are few risks for children who use online services. Teenagers are particularly at risk because they often use the computer unsupervised and because they are more likely than younger children to participate in online discussions regarding companionship, relationships, or sexual activity.

There are risks for your children online but these risks are no different from the risks your children face in everyday life. And, just as in real life, it is impossible to safeguard or isolate children from everything we don't want them to see, know, or come in contact with. However, in today's electronic society, it is also important to provide children with access to the tremendous resources available online.

There has been a great deal of discussion by the media, legislators, educators, and parents about how to control children's use of the Internet and online services. While approaches of the parties differ, all unanimously agree that the cornerstone of any control system has to be a set of guidelines. Guidelines must be set up by parents in cooperation with their children to define the playing field—what's in bounds and what's out— what the rules and penalties associated are; when there is practice and when lights out should be. No coach would dream of letting players run practice nor would he skip the game and hope for the best. Neither should you let your "players" take the field without guidance and oversight to assure that your "team" always wins.

This chapter outlines how to set these rules up for your house and provides ideas about what the rules might include. I wish I could tell you that everything in this chapter is original, moreover I wish I was smart enough to have thought of it all, but in addition to the guidelines we teach parents at Safety Net, I have included guidelines put forth by a number of other sources. While they all say basically the same things, each one has a little different twist that I thought might be helpful. I have also provided a sample agreement you can use to formalize your family's guidelines.

Laying the Foundation

The fact that inappropriate material is available online is not a reason to avoid using online services. To tell children to stop using these services would be like telling them to not attend college because students are sometimes victimized on campus. A better solution might be to teach children what dangers exist and how to avoid them. To develop street smarts so they can steer clear of potentially dangerous situations. The first step in developing street smarts is establishing ground rules that will allow children to begin their online experience without trouble.

Begin the process by starting an ongoing dialogue with your children. Parents and kids need to talk to each other about actions that might be considered offensive, why kids should let parents know if they feel uneasy about a situation online, and why some areas are not the places parents want them to visit.

There is also a need for parents to provide continuing supervision. Children mean well but let's face it, they are kids and curiosity may lead them to places where they should not be. What parent hasn't heard "well, Johnny did it" as the reason for errant behaviors? Similarly, kids may imitate the actions of others online.

Finally, parents must be involved themselves. Ask your kids to help you find things online that you might be interested in. Perhaps a trip to the Smithsonian, NASCAR's homepage, or check out last night's sport scores. Encourage family involvement by picking a topic and having each member of the family—that means mom and dad too—find some related topics online. One evening have everyone show each other what they have found about the topic of the week. Last, let your children know you are interested in what they are doing and will help them if they want your assistance.

Plan a time for a family discussion to mutually establish guidelines for who, what, when, where, and how much online services should cost. Write these rules down and post them at the computer as a reminder of what everyone agreed to.

WHO

Meeting new people is an exciting and fun part of being online. As a result of online services, the concept of pen pals has expanded to include virtually any country around the world. Because the vast majority of online communication is positive and without danger, don't discourage your children's interaction with others. Do be aware however, that not everyone online is harmless.

○ **Talk with your children about interaction online.** You don't want to scare them, but they need to be aware of what constitutes inappropriate behavior. Encourage your children to discuss with you any problems they may encounter.

○ **Teach your children about strangers in the online world.** Here again, the rule of thumb I use is: *If you wouldn't do it in real life, don't do it online.* The concept of a stranger is a particularly tough one online as nearly everyone is a stranger in the usual sense of the word. An illustration may be helpful. Suzy is playing at the park and meets Michelle on the swings. Michelle's mother comes over and starts talking to the girls and offers them drinks. Is Michelle's mother a stranger? Clearly she is a stranger. But there is a significantly greater threat from the man in the station wagon lurking in the parking lot over the threat that Michelle's mother poses.

○ **Explain that not everyone online always tells the truth about who they are.** People may say they are older or younger than they really are, they may claim to be of a different gender, or they may pose as a figure of authority to get kids to do something they shouldn't.

○ **Tell your children, regardless of who asks, to *never* give out their name, address, or phone number.** First names are OK since it would be hard to find a child only by their first name. Also talk about exercising caution about such information as the schools they attend, mom and dad's names or occupations; in fact, I even encourage my kids not to tell others online what city they live in. You may want to exercise some discretion here but protecting this type of information is just good preventive medicine.

○ **Tell your children not to give out their email address without your permission.** At this time, there is no way for others to get your email address unless you give it to them. For that reason, selectivity will prevent your child from exposure to harassing or inappropriate material on email.

○ **Regardless of who asks for it, *never* give your password to anybody online.** Be advised that numerous scam artists pose as service administrators and ask you to verify your password online. These are crooks looking to utilize your account for access and should not only be denied the information but also reported to your service provider. No service provider will ever ask you for your password online. If you ever have doubts simply ask them to call you back at the phone number that is part of your service records.

Just a word on selecting passwords. As part of setting up service, installing blocking software, and many other activities, you will be asked to input a password. In order to keep your passwords secure, from both fraudulent users as well as your kids, the password should consist of a minimum of five characters and use both letters and numbers. When selecting a password get creative. Do not use commonly known combinations like:

○ your birthday

○ son's/daughter's name or birthday

○ favorite color

○ dog's name

○ license plate number

○ mother's maiden name

○ social security number

○ anniversary date

○ phone number or bank PIN

Warning

One last word of caution on passwords. Do not write them down or tell your children your passwords. By selecting your passwords carefully and protecting them from unwanted use, you can remain in control of who, what, when, where, and how as it relates to your computer, your personal information, and the Internet.

○ **Make it clear that unless they have your permission, kids are not to send photographs to others online.** If anyone asks for pictures, your children should let you know immediately.

○ **Agree that your children will never arrange to meet with someone in person** unless you know about it, it is in a public place, and you are with them when they meet the person.

The following list was taken from the National Center for Missing and Exploited Children pamphlet *Child Safety on the Information Highway* . To obtain a copy call the center at (800) THE-LOST, (800) 843-5678.

Guidelines for Parents

By taking responsibility for your children's online computer use, parents can greatly minimize any potential risks of being online. Make it a family rule to:

○ Never give out identifying information—home address, school name, or telephone number—in a public message such as chat or bulletin boards, and be sure you're dealing with someone that both you and your child know and trust before giving it out via email. Think carefully before revealing any personal information such as age, marital status, or financial information. Consider using a pseudonym or unlisting your child's name if your service allows it.

❍ Get to know the services your child uses. If you don't know how to log on, get your child to show you. Find out what types of information it offers and whether there are ways for parents to block out objectionable material.

❍ Never allow a child to arrange a face-to-face meeting with another computer user without parental permission. If a meeting is arranged, make the first one in a public spot, and be sure to accompany your child.

❍ Never respond to messages or bulletin board items that are suggestive, obscene, belligerent, threatening, or make you feel uncomfortable. Encourage your children to tell you if they encounters such messages. If you or your child receives a message that is harassing, of a sexual nature, or threatening, forward a copy of the message to your service provider and ask for their assistance.

❍ If a meeting is arranged, make the first one in a public spot.

❍ Should you become aware of the transmission, use, or viewing of child pornography while online, immediately report this to the National Center for Missing and Exploited Children by calling (800) 843-5678. You should also notify your online service.

❍ Remember that people online may not be who they seem. Because you can't see or even hear the person it would be easy for someone to misrepresent him- or herself. Thus, someone indicating that "she" is a "12-year-old girl" could in reality be a 40-year-old man.

❍ Remember that everything you read online may not be true. Any offer that's "too good to be true" probably is. Be very careful about any offers that involve your coming to a meeting or having someone visit your house.

○ Set reasonable rules and guidelines for computer use by your children. Discuss these rules and post them near the computer as a reminder. Remember to monitor their compliance with these rules, especially when it comes to the amount of time your children spend on the computer. A child or teenager's excessive use of online services or bulletin boards, especially late at night, may be a clue that there is a potential problem. Remember that personal computers and online services should not be used as electronic baby-sitters.

○ Be sure to make this a family activity. Consider keeping the computer in a family room rather than the child's bedroom. Get to know their "online friends" just as you get to know all of their other friends.

WHAT

○ **Show your children how to connect with the service or services you use.** Have your children get you before they try to change anything in the set up or configuration area.

○ **Show your children how to disconnect from your service provider** and stress the importance of disconnecting when they are finished or are idle for long periods of time. This will free up the phone line for other uses and is particularly important if you are using the existing voice line for online access. Disconnecting is also especially important if your service provider does not provide an automatic disconnect feature that will terminate your connection after a predetermined period of nonuse. Failure to disconnect in this situation may result in charges from your service provider for every hour online resulting in a huge phone bill at the end of the month.

A recent seminar participant explained how they had gotten rid of a particular online service as the result of an astronomical month end bill. Her daughter had logged on to the service when she arrived home one afternoon. In the heat of helping with dinner and attending an engagement for the evening, she had forgotten to log off. Returning home late that night she slipped into bed without a second thought. The next morning she arose, dressed, ate breakfast, and was off to school. It was not until the next afternoon, some 24 hours later, that the daughter realized she had not logged off and had indeed been charged almost $75.00 for her forgetfulness. Have your children demonstrate they know how to disconnect and never feel ashamed about checking on them at the end of a particular session.

○ **Lead by example and demonstrate for your children how you expect them to interact online.** Teach your children the importance of "netiquette" and positive communication. Set clear expectations as they relate to: 1) posting to "newsgroups" or other areas where the public will read their input, 2) email they send to others, and 3) their conduct in chat rooms or IRC chat sessions. Be aware that others online will not follow common courtesy and advise your children to mind their manners regardless of what others are doing. The rule of thumb I stress with youngsters is: *Do not put something on the Internet that you wouldn't want in the headlines of your home town newspaper the next day or that you would be ashamed of your mother or father reading.*

Netiquette

The rule about limiting what you say online applies to adults too. A recent client told me how one of his colleagues, having had multiple incidents of poor performance with his assistant, had sent an email to human resources indicating his intention to fire her. He did not realize until after the fact, that he had not only sent the memo to human resources but had also copied his assistant.

○ Let your children know that the use of your service provider is a privilege you are offering them, not a right. Put a value on this privilege by tying it to allowances or finishing chores. One way you may want to increase this sense of value is to determine how online usage will be split between school use and play and asking the kids to pay for the percentage of time the service is used for play.

A Point Value System

Another way to add value to online time without linking it to money is to develop a point system. The point system is based on the premise that mom and dad will pay for time online as long as the family can collectively show that the presence of the online service is creating positive results. Those results are measured by the accumulation of points. Points are awarded for various tasks accomplished on the computer. Each month the slate is reset to zero and accumulation starts again. Some ideas about actions that add or subtract points are shown below:

Adders

○ Completion of homework assignments

○ Raising a grade a level (from from a *B* to an *A*)

○ Doing research

○ Finding new topics of interest to the family

- ○ Setting up next week's family night on the computer
- ○ Finding bargains
- ○ Finding new recipes (that don't kill anybody)
- ○ Reducing magazine subscriptions by using online versions
- ○ Using an online encyclopedia (instead of buying a hardbound set)
- ○ Tracking the investment portfolio
- ○ Balancing the checkbook
- ○ Pulling email from home so mom and dad get home earlier

SUBTRACTERS

- ○ Failure to complete chores
- ○ Failing grades
- ○ Disrespect
- ○ Violation of ground rules
- ○ Budget violations
- ○ Too much time playing games

Each action may have the same number of points associated with it or you may make school related actions and negative actions worth more points so there is a greater incentive to focus on the things that gain (or not take away) the greatest number of points. These are just a few suggestions. Modify the list to meet your particular households needs. Set the number of points required to keep the online service high enough that it will challenge kids to stay involved in the activity and look for ways to increase the tool's value in your home.

○ **Check your service to see if there are specific areas for kids.** (See Chapter 5, Selecting a Service Provider, to determine which providers offer these types of services.) These areas are monitored for content and often have very strict rules for use. If your kids use these areas, go over the rules with your children and reinforce that they are expected to follow these rules.

○ **Make sure you know your children's passwords and online ID/names.** There are two reasons for this: 1) If you know their password, you can check on what they are doing online. Remember that kids need space and privacy to grow but explain to them that in circumstances where their well being is at stake, not all privacy can be respected. 2) Children often forget their passwords and ID/names. I recently read one of the universal truths of online services and it went something like this: If your children have their own passwords, no one, including the child, will know it. However, if your family has only one password, the whole neighborhood will know it.

○ **Kids love to download and try out new software and games.** Help them to understand the difference between the software and shareware. Software labeled as freeware or public domain is exactly that, free! However, software labeled shareware is not. If kids download a shareware program, they may try the software for a specified period of time. Then, if they want to keep it they just send in the required payment. If they decide not to keep it, simply delete the program from the computer.

○ **Be aware of what your kids are doing online.** As any of you who have been online know, it is easy to get sidetracked. This is even more true when what you are supposed to be doing is homework. That is not to say that getting sidetracked is always bad, in fact chatting in chat rooms, or just surfin' the net looking for fun often leads to additional learning. However, your kids could be spending too much time in game areas, or letting time online interfere with getting schoolwork done or finishing chores around the house.

Online Manners (Netiquette) for Students[1]

1. Check your letters, email, and writings before you send or post them online. Sometimes other people may misunderstand what you mean to say. If you are writing to, or doing a project involving students from other countries, you need to be sensitive to cultural differences.

2. Only post online or send via email items that your family considers to be in good taste.

3. Don't type in all CAPS. Use of all capital letters appears like shouting and seems rude.

4. If someone sends you email that is nasty or offensive, don't reply. Don't pull yourself down to the level of that person. Forward offensive email to your service and let the service handle it.

5. Just because others can't see you and may not know you, doesn't give you the right to act improperly or to say or print things that you wouldn't normally do. Use your common sense.

6. Although you should not give out personal information to those you meet online, you also shouldn't fabricate stories about who you are.

7. When joining a chat session or live discussion, take the time to understand what is being discussed before entering the conversation. Don't just jump in and ask why your disk drive isn't working, how old everyone is, or if it's snowing in Minneapolis. If there is a topic for the discussion, make sure your comments relate to the discussion.

8. During live online conferences, there are often rules of protocol. Especially when lots of people participate in a session, protocol keeps the conversation from degenerating into chaos. Partial Protocol usually means that if you want to ask a question, you type in a **?** and wait until you are called on to send your question. If you want to make a comment, you can just jump in with comments as long as they pertain to the subject. If you are not finished with what you are typing, but run out of space in the text area, type three periods ... and send. Then begin typing again and send. When you are finished with your question or comment, type **GA** (Go Ahead) so that the next person knows when to begin. For *Full Protocol*, you must type **!** when you want to make a comment and wait until you are asked by the session moderator to make your comment.

9. Appreciate the volunteers who help with online services. Many of the people directing sessions for young people are educators, parents, and students who are not paid (except perhaps in extra online time) for the enormous amount of work they do. Volunteer to help yourself. No matter how old you are or how experienced you are with being online, you can help with live discussions (chats), in bulletin board discussion areas, by sharing information with others, etc. Don't let others do all the work for you. Many online services depend upon the help of members.

WHEN

Market research tells us that the average teen spends more time on the computer than in front of the television. With that being the case it is not unreasonable to expect your child to be online 5 to 10 hours per week. With several children that could amount to as much as 80 to 100 hours per month online! Setting limits for your children on the amount of time they may spend in online activities will help them learn to make efficient use of their time online and maintain a balance of activities in their lives.

○ **Discuss with your kids when the computer may be used and when it can't** and more particularly when they may go online. Create specific times when homework and studying are to be done. If you are using a service that charges more during peak hours (usually business hours), you may want to establish specific off-peak times for your children's online usage to manage costs. But be sure to define what time is lights out. Many times parents have shared stories of getting up in the middle of the night to find their child online engulfed in a chat session, a game, or worse.

○ **Establish limits for the number of hours per day and number of hours per week that kids can be online.** This will help kids make efficient use of their time online. Remember to be flexible here as there may be times when a little more time may be required to finish research for a school paper or a particularly interesting chat room or forum is just winding up.

○ **If you are using your home's telephone line to make your online connection, remind kids that when they are online no one else can either make or receive calls.** One way to manage this situation is to assign usage times so the phone is free during those hours when it must be available for either incoming or outgoing calls.

ONLINE USAGE TIME TABLE

At our house, we use a simple form that shows what hours the computer may be used for online connections and whose turn it is to use it during those hours. Each person (including mom and dad) has a color and we simply color in each block with the color of the person whose turn it is to go online. Red indicates that the computer is not to be used during that hour. This simple tool has virtually eliminated the problem of "when" in our home.

		1	2	3	4	5	6	7	8	9	10	11	12	1	2	3	4	5	6	7	8	9	10	11	12
Sun																									
Mon																									
Tues																									
Wed																									
Thur																									
Fri																									
Sat																									

Figure 6.1 *Online usage time table.*

WHERE

○ **Talk with your children about places they may go online.** Although the specifics will vary depending on their age, knowledge, interests, and abilities, you need to make it clear that certain areas are off limits. A number of publications offer suggestions about children's sites that range from the adventurous to the absurd. Preview these chat groups, web pages, and newsgroups to see if they are appropriate and make a list of the good ones to use as a guide. We make a habit of introducing a couple of new sites every other week or so and taking away the less used ones. A starter list for various age groups is provided in Appendix D. This list is by no means all inclusive but does list some established, time-tested sites. Additional sites may be found in the "Kids Only" section of our home page at **http://www.safesurfing.com**.

○ **One of the most effective things you can do as a parent is to guide your children to the positive.** Work with children to show them exciting and fun places to explore and they will be much less prone to wander into inappropriate areas. This is especially true for younger children who are still prone to mimicking what mom and dad does. This will obviously be less effective with older kids and teens who will want to explore freely but a little reverse psychology might work here. Ask them to note the cool new sites and help to guide you there. This is certainly no panacea but the benefits of creating good habits early will pay large dividends later on.

○ **Encourage your children to participate in chat groups and discussions that are monitored.** These groups usually have a volunteer who watches what is going on in the chat room and chaperones. If a particular participant is exceptionally rude or vulgar or discussing inappropriate topics, the monitor will usually warn the person once and then ban them from the chat room. This ban may last hours, days, or forever. Final recourse for participants who do not conform to the rules of monitored chat groups can be denial of service by their service provider.

How Much

○ **Talk with your kids about online expenses.** They should understand that the use of online services is not free, even if they are accessing the Internet.

○ **Discuss with your kids the costs associated with connecting to bulletin boards (BBS) via long distance calls.** Not only do many of these BBSs have per minute access charges but you must also pay the long distance charges as well. Help your kids to identify BBSs that are within your local calling area as a way of getting a handle on these costs.

○ If you connect with a service that charges on an hourly basis you may want to do the following (see Chapter 5, Choosing a Service Provider):

○ **Make sure you are using a high speed modem (28.8 Kbps) and have configured your system to take advantage of the speed.** This will result in less time online to search, open documents, send email or download documents and subsequently lower costs.

- ○ **Teach your children to download mail and read it offline.** Likewise, show them how to use the software to compose email offline and then go online only to send their message.

- ○ **Show your children how to post or send the work they prepared offline once they log on.**

- ○ **Learn how to use favorite places or similar areas where your computer records the address of frequently used services or sites so that at the click of a mouse you can quickly return to them.** Learn how to use keywords to shorten search times and quickly jump from one topic to the next. These will shorten time online by taking you directly to those areas you use most frequently.

- ○ **Explore ways to save time online as a family by sharing time online with brother and sisters or learning to type faster.** How many others can you and your family think of?

- ○ **Discussing costs and establishing budgets is a great way to teach children the value of a dollar and learn budgeting skills that will serve them well later on in life.** If your children earn an allowance, you might ask that they pay for the time they spend online playing games (or some portion of it). Alternatively, you might link time online to the completion of certain chores or assignments. The key to making this type of link successful is the presence of penalties for not living up to the family's agreement. If they fail to finish their chores or do not live up to their end of the bargain, enforcement of these penalties will help to bring about a change in behavior patterns.

Acceptable Use Policies and Parental Agreements

To date, schools have been relatively effective at controlling access to inappropriate materials in large part due to the fact that access has been limited enough that teachers can effectively oversee use. This will change with the introduction of widespread access. However, schools have also taken advantage of kids' eagerness to use the Internet and have created *acceptable use policy statements* that lay out the ground rules for which students are allowed to use online access at school and the consequences if they violate those guidelines.

These types of agreements, and the success educators have had with them, were in part responsible for our suggesting that parents sit down with their children and create a similar policy or agreement for the home.

During a seminar when I suggest that an agreement will guide a child's usage, it is easy to see which parents have teens and which do not. The parents of the teens are always the ones who at this point are looking at me as if I have lost my mind! "Agreements won't work with teens" are the sentiments I often here echoed from parents. Admittedly, a solid agreement will be more effective with younger children and will have more lasting effects in shaping future usage. However, coupled with blocking software (see Chapter 8) to enforce the agreement in your absence, and *enforced* consequences for violations, an agreement can be a powerful tool for teens as well.

The teeth of the agreement are the consequences that take advantage of kids being so enamored with being online. As parents of the television age, we are well aware of the angst caused when we restrict TV time. Or for those of you with teenage drivers, take away the keys for a day or two. The corrective effect will be much the same for your children and the Internet. In a very short period of time, kids will develop friends online that they routinely chat with and develop favorite web sites that keep them updated on what's happening about a particular show or topic. In short, their dependence on the Internet or other online services grows to a point that enforced limitation of use is an effective deterrent to inappropriate behavior.

At many seminars, kids are either present or in adjoining areas with other activities. At the end of the seminar, I am always overwhelmed at the number of kids inquiring with their parents before they have even left the facility, "Can we go online now?" If you have any doubts, just tell your kids that you are looking into getting online and note the reaction.

CONTENTS OF THE AGREEMENT

The contents of your agreement should reflect the ground rules you have established during your discussions with your kids. The agreement should be studied in detail by your child, signed by you and your child and posted near your computer where it can be clearly viewed. A copy of the agreement found on our homepage at **http://www.safesurfing.com/contract** is shown on the next page. You may print the contract as it is or copy it into your word processor and amend to it to reflect the ground rules you and your kids have agreed on.

Parent's Ground Rules

In addition to the ground rules you should establish with your kids, as the parent of a online user you may want to consider the following as ground rules by which to conduct your online actions so as to teach by example:

○ Demonstrate the things you want your kids to do when you are online.

○ Become familiar with the literature that came with your service provider's software and the tools available to you.

○ Seek the advice and counsel of other computer users in your area.

○ Establish open communication with your children about things to beware of in the real world and the parallel risk online.

Sample Agreement

OFFICIAL INTERNET CONTRACT

I, _____, agree to abide by the following rules that are necessary for my safe use and enjoyment of the Internet:

- ◯ I will not surf the Internet for more than _____ hours per day, _____ hours per week, or _____ hours per month.

- ◯ I will keep my parents informed of all my activities on the Internet at all times.

- ◯ I will never give out personal information — including my phone number, address, or the name and location of my school.

- ◯ I will avoid unpleasant situations. If I find myself in such a situation, I will logoff the Internet and report it to my parents.

- ◯ I will always be myself.

- ◯ I will always stick to my budget.

- ◯ I will always express myself in a cool and calm manner.

- ◯ I will always treat others as I would want to be treated myself.

- ◯ I will always help newbies if they are having problems surfing the Net.

- ◯ I will always use my common sense.

○   I will treat everyone on the Internet with respect.

○   I will always share any good ideas or information that I have.

○   I will be an active and useful member of Cyberspace.

○   I will inform my parents if I come across any information that makes me feel uncomfortable or weird.

○   I will never agree to get together with someone I "meet" on the Internet, without my parents' permission. If I get permission, my parents will come with me and we will only meet in a public place.

○   I will not visit areas on the Internet that have been set off-limits to me.

If I do not follow these rules and guidelines, I realize that my Internet or other privileges will be taken away and I will not be able to surf the Internet for a period of _____ days/hours.

Child: _____   Date:_____

Parent: _____   Date: _____

The bottom line is it is up to *you*, as parents and educators, to set reasonable guidelines for your children's usage of online services. Discuss the rules and post them near the computer. Remember to monitor their compliance with the rules, especially as they relate to time online. By taking responsibility for your children's online computer use, you can greatly minimize the potential risks involved in being online.

My rules for Online Safety

○ I will not give out personal information such as my address, telephone number, parents' work address/telephone number, or the name and location of my school without my parents' permission.

○ I will tell my parents right away if I come across any information that makes me feel uncomfortable.

○ I will never agree to get together with someone I "meet" online without first checking with my parents. If my parents agree to the meeting, I will be sure that it is in a public place and bring my mother or father along.

○ I will never send a person my picture or anything else without first checking with my parents.

○ I will not respond to any messages that are mean or in any way make me feel uncomfortable. It is not my fault if I get a message like that. If I do I will tell my parents right away so that they can contact the online service.

○ I will talk with my parents so that we can set up rules for going online. We will decide upon the time of day that I can be online, the length of time I can be online, and appropriate areas for me to visit. I will not access other areas or break these rules without their permission.[2]

FOOTNOTES

[1](Marsh, Merle 1995) *Everything You Need to Know About the Information Highway.* Reprinted with permission from the Computer Learning Foundation, P.O. Box 60007, Palo Alto, CA 94306-0007. Computer Learning Foundation, Palo Alto, CA

2 'My Rules for Online Safety' are from *Child Safety on the Information Highway* by Lawrence J. Magid. This information is reprinted with the permission of the National Center for Missing and Exploited Children (NCMEC). Copyright 1994 NCMEC. All rights reserved.

Getting Involved

In general, the parenting skills that apply to the real world also apply while online. Teach your children right from wrong by example, guide their actions, participate in the things they do and correct them when they are wrong—none of these are unfamiliar. Yet when it comes to doing these things online, all too often parents freeze up, back away and throw their hands up in the air. Perhaps you have seen some of the "warning signs" that might indicate a problem exists:

- "Don't come in right now... just a minute" is a common response to your knock on the door.
- Quickly changing screens when you walk into the room.
- Unusually late hours on computer.
- Charges on your credit cards that are of questionable origin. Penny's Porn Shop is usually billed as something much less obvious.

In this chapter, you will find an alternative to throwing your hands up—getting involved. Not in a remote way but hands on, step-by-step, so you will know what your kids are talking about and most importantly, that you can do it yourself. Specifically you will get more comfortable with getting online and what to do once you get there. Finally, there is a series of activities you may want to undertake with your kids.

This chapter is meant to be a hands-on experience so there are lots of instructions and pictures of what the screens will look like. Don't panic if your screen doesn't look exactly like the one shown, we may have used a different version of software or Macintosh instead of Windows. If you read the text and poke around in the pull-down menus (try clicking on those words in the gray bar across the top of your screen and you will see why they call them that), you will get right back on track. I encourage you to read the chapter once and then sit down in front of your computer, with the book nearby, and try each activity. At the end of your second time through the chapter, I am sure you will be ready to sit down with your kids and begin to get involved. You are most likely even farther behind in the age of information than you will ever know. However, after reading this chapter, you can rest assured that most people are even further behind than you!

Getting Comfortable

To be involved, no matter how scary it may be, sooner or later you are going to have to get online. The two biggest objections to getting online that we hear from parents are:

○ I might break something.

○ I don't know how.

These comments are driven by lack of knowledge and fear of the unknown. I cannot say often enough that the chances of you damaging your computer by logging on to an online service are exactly two—slim and none! If you are one of those who has never been online before, take this book, go to your computer and follow along. In no time you will be up and running.

By now you have probably selected a service provider. If not, selecting a service provider and detailed instructions for getting signed onto those services are found in Chapter 5, Choosing a Service Provider. You should turn to that page now, determine what type of service provider best suits your needs, and get signed up.

The examples shown in this chapter use a national Internet Service Provider, NETCOM, and for the most part we use the NetCruiser "browser." In some cases we will demonstrate other browsers for clarity. Regardless of which service provider or browser you ultimately choose, the instructions here are fairly generic and will look very similar to the one you select. The idea here is for you to see how easy it is to start the engine that will take you down the information superhighway.

Note Remember—a browser is just a computer program that allows you to access the Internet. Netscape Navigator is the most popular browser but many exist. Each commercial service provider also has their own proprietary browser.

Logging On

Start by double-clicking the Program Manager (or hard drive icon on a Macintosh) or click **Start** in Windows 95. Double click the folder that has your access software in it (it is probably named after your service provider) to open it, and click the program icon to start the program (see Figure 7.1).

When the logon screen appears, type in your **user name** and **password** and click **Logon.** (See Figure 7.2) Some programs may insert your user name for you and all you have to do is type in your password. You will hear a dial tone and then the modem dialing. Then that familiar screeching noise and you are online! (See Figure 7.3.)

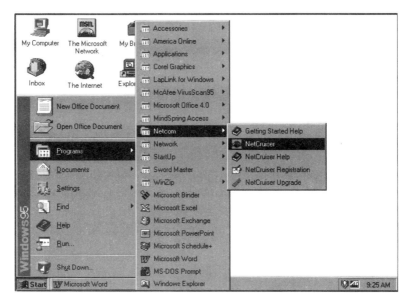

Figure 7.1 From the Program Manager double-click on your
service provider's icon to launch the program.

Figure 7.2 Tab between fields to enter your User Name and Password; double-click **Logon**.

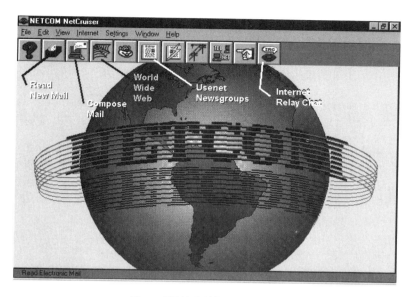

Figure 7.3 *Voila! You are online!*

See, that wasn't so hard. And as you try it more often you will get very adept at logging on and getting right to those places you really want to go.

NO LUCK?

If for some reason you can't connect on your first try, don't blame yourself, and immediately start changing things. Many times a failure to connect is the result of noisy phone lines, high traffic volume, or any number of other technical things. Start by checking the telephone connections at the wall, the modem, and your computer. If those are in order, walk away for a few minutes and try again. The idea here is that if you start changing things and it is indeed the service provider's problem, you must now try to remember what you changed and put it back the way it was. If after two or three tries you are still having problems, give the customer service number a call and let them earn their keep.

Having conquered the hardest part, you are now poised to fall into the endless world of online information. Go ahead and read on.

Getting Familiar

One of the most satisfying parts of our seminars is the comments parents make as we conclude. Not about our teaching style or presentation skills but rather about the awesome power of the Internet. We frequently hear, "I knew there was a lot there but I had no idea how easy it is to get to," or "Now I know why my kids are so excited—I am too."

One of the greatest resources to help you get familiar with the world online is already in your house and is probably free—your own child. What better way to become involved than to let your child teach you. Once you are familiar and your confidence builds, you should do some exploring on your own to understand the good and the bad that exists. But as you start out, do so as a family and enjoy the bonds you build on one of the few occasions your child will get to teach you something.

For those of you who won't humble yourselves, try a local computer user's group or just stop by the school and ask the computer specialist for some help. You will find these individuals are more than willing to enlighten a parent because you will ultimately make their job much easier. One final caution when going online the first several times is to set aside plenty of time. Several two hour blocks ought to be enough time to teach even a newbie the ropes of access and navigating the Internet, but don't short change yourself, the result will only be even greater frustration.

THE STARTING LINE

If you have logged on with a commercial service provider, the first screen will contain a number of different topics you can choose from (see Figure 7.4.)

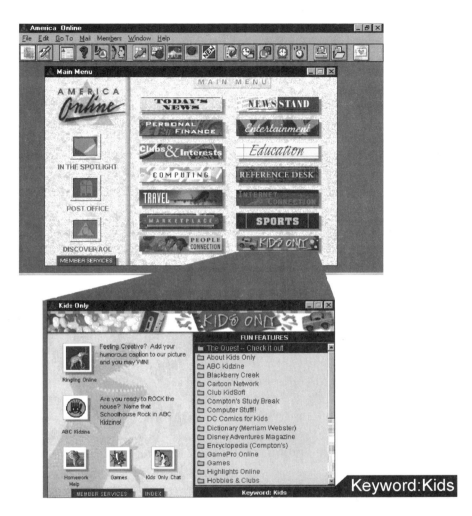

Figure 7.4 AOL's Main Menu is a good example of the startup screen you will find with most commercial service providers .

These are by no means all of the topics from which you can choose, just some of the most popular ones. When you click your mouse on one of these topics, it will change the screen and a submenu or table of contents for the topic you chose will appear. This may happen several times before you get to the actual information you want but be patient, it is worth it. If you want to get back to the beginning, use the **Go To** pull-down menu and click on the **Main Menu**. Virtually all of the commercial service providers use some arrangement of *key words* that allow you to type in that word and *jump* immediately to that screen. For instance, the key word for our example is **KIDS**. By clicking on **GO TO** and typing the keyword **KIDS** in, we could immediately jump to that set of information.

In addition to the areas of interest on each page, across the top of all provider's screens are a number of icons that will lead you to other resources—chat rooms, the Internet, email (see Figure 7.5).

Figure 7.5 Though each provider will use its own icons, they will all resemble those on the AOL menu bar shown above .

If you have selected an Internet service provider, the first screen you encounter may look a little different. The reason for this is simple. Each service provider is an independent company with its own product development group and customer service group who create and assemble the *access screen* from the hundreds of software products available for accessing the various parts of the Internet. The result is hundreds of startup screen configurations. Figure 7.6 is a depiction of NETCOM's access screen and that of Mindspring, a large service provider in the Southeast. Each has a button for the WWW, email, Newsgroups, and IRC Chat Groups among others.

What may at first seem very confusing is in fact one of the very powerful reasons I strongly recommend people using an ISP over commercial service providers. The ability to choose between products that suit your needs can only be found with ISPs who have their own access software. If you don't like the particular mail reader AOL or CompuServe provides you have two choices get used to it or change providers. With an ISP you can simply change the program to one you like better—and most of those programs can be found on the Internet for free. Remember, while it may seem chaotic at first, the Internet is designed to be a free-form environment where changes can be made quickly and easily—one of the powerful features of the Internet!

Figure 7.6 Each ISP offers their own startup screen but all achieve the same task.

To move from area to area on an ISP you simply use icons (see Figure 7.6) just as you would the ones on the title bar of a commercial service provider. One other powerful positive on using the Internet is the fact that while the commercial service providers make a wide array of options available on their starting pages, their starting pages are based on what they perceive to be most useful or at best what the largest number of subscribers ask for. This may or may not have anything to do with your interests. On the Internet, you will have the flexibility of creating your own homepage that will have only the items of interest to you—the WWW site, chat groups, and newsgroups you participate in most commonly. We will talk about how to select someone else's homepage or create one of your own later in this chapter.

Some Exercises to Get your Feet Wet

Before we get started, call a friend who is online and ask them to send you an email message. Remember, you will need to give them your email address so write it down before you go to the phone. While you are at it get their email address as well, we will send them a note to let them know we are online.

Exercise 1: Connect to the service and explore the startup screen

Even though you may already be logged on go ahead and quit your session. What's that? You don't know how to quit? OK—here is a little hint. You quit your online session just like any other program.

- ○ Move your cursor to the "square" in the top right hand corner of your screen and click.
- ○ You will be prompted to see if you really want to quit; so click **OK**.

Now, get back online. That's right, get back online.

Very good! Just wanted to see if you remembered how. Now this time when the first screen comes up, sit back and survey the possibilities. Take your time and read the descriptions. Try out some of the icons if you want. In many cases if you position the pointer of your mouse on a particular topic or picture, a "help balloon" will appear with additional information about the topic.

Exercise 2: Do some initial exploring

Since you are already online, let's start with something fun. Once again, nothing you do here will hurt you or the computer so I want you to give every button and icon that is on your screen a try. If you get somewhere and can't get back, just go to the file pull-down menu and click **Quit**.

○ Click on the **World Wide Web (WWW)**.

○ At the top of the screen will be a box that either says Location, URL, or has a string of characters starting with http://www.... Highlight whatever is there and then type **http://www.yahoo.com/** (make sure you type this in all lower case letters). Press **Return**.

○ Scroll down the screen (Figure 7.7) until you see a topic in "blue text" that interests you. click on the blue text.

○ If your startup screen is one that has a number of topics displayed on it, click one of those topics instead of going to the World Wide Web.

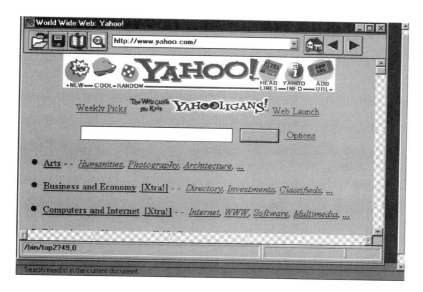

Figure 7.7 Yahoo's screen should look like this—Go ahead, click on the blue text.

Try out several different topics to get familiar with how they work and how to maneuver between screens. When you are done with the Web, try the icons in the menu bar. These icons will often lead to other services as well as shortcuts to printing, help, saving, and opening files. Don't be afraid to try them all out just to see how they work. If you don't like what you see just click **Cancel** and you will go back to where you just came from.

Exercise 3: Send a Friend a Note

Once you begin sending notes to people online you will be amazed at how much more you will communicate. Since my parents got a computer, we send messages two to three times a week rather than two to three per month.

○ Click on the icon on your screen (usually in the menu bar) for mail. It might be a mailbox, a flying letter, or something as simple as email.

○ A screen will open that will have the header—To, From, or CC— and a place for typing a message. There may be other options on the screen but ignore these for now. You may want to play with them later.

○ Press the **Tab** key until the cursor is in the box labeled *To:*.

○ Type in the email address of the friend you called earlier. Remember these addresses are case sensitive so use caps and small letters exactly as they were given to you and don't forget to put the @ sign in the right place. For instance, if you were going to send me an email you would type in **jmc@mindspring.com**.

○ Press **Tab** until the cursor is in the box labeled **Subject:** and type a brief description of what your note is about (e.g., **Hey—I'm Online**).

○ Press **Tab** until the cursor is in the large box and type the body of your letter.

○ Click **Send** to deliver your mail.

Your message has been sent—no stamps, no mailboxes, no waiting. By the time you pick up the phone to see if your friend received the message it will already be there.

Exercise 4: Read Your Mail

Now that you have sent a message, let's read the one your friend sent you.

○ Click on the button or pull-down menus that read something like **New Mail, Mailbox - In,** or **Read New Mail**.

○ A list of unread messages will appear on the screen. Double-click on one and the message will open and you can read what your friend wrote.

Exercise 5: Reply to the Message

○ In the menu bar of your email program you may see a Reply button, a U-turn shaped arrow, or some other icon that indicates the ability to respond to mail sent to you. If not, look in the pull-down menus and you will find a Reply command. Click on that button.

○ Below your friend's message type in a line of dashes, asterisks or some other delineator between your message and theirs. Below this separator, type in your response to your friend's message and click **Send** as if you were sending a new message.

Way to go! You are using email. I think you will agree, this makes "snail mail" look positively antiquated.

A COMMON COURTESY

You may want to delete all but the first line or two of your friend's message prior to sending the reply so the length of the message does not become unwieldy. I usually put a row of dashes after the original message and then type my reply using the original message to reference back to. Then, just before I send it I highlight the body of the original text and delete all but a couple of lines, just so they will know what I am responding to.

Exercise 6: Usenet Newsgroups

For those of you using commercial service providers, until now you have stayed within the confines of your provider's services. This exercise will take you onto the Internet and all the excitement that awaits you there.

○ Click on the **Internet** icon in the menu bar. (A warning screen will most likely ask you to confirm your intent to enter the Internet through your service providers gateway. Click on **OK**.)

○ It may take as long as several minutes to make the connection or you may get a busy signal but be patient and try again if necessary, until you get a response that indicates you are connected to the Internet. A screen will appear with several new icons for; **World Wide Web**; **Newsgroups**, **IRC Chat** and perhaps a few others.

○ Click on the icon for **Newsgroups.**

○ A screen that looks something like Figure 7.8 will then appear.

Newsgroups are those areas where you can read and reply to people's comments on a variety of topics that range from anthropology to zoology (and many less desirable places in between). At any given time there may be as many as several thousand Newsgroups active so be patient if it takes few minutes to download all the information you are looking for.

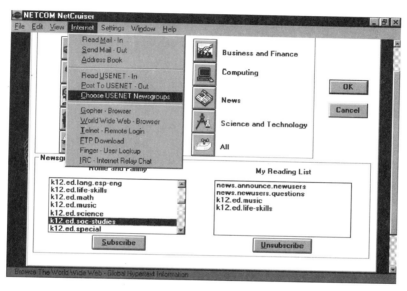

Figure 7.8 Using icons or pull-down menus, add Newsgroups to your reading list by clicking on the list on the left.

○ Click on the **Newsgroups** icon on your startup screen.

○ Click the **Subscribe** button or use the pull-down menus to get to the **Select Newsgroup** command.

Note

Subscribing to a newsgroup is a bit misleading. Most people think of subscriptions as something you pay a monthly fee for (like magazines). But for Newsgroups it is just a way of saying "join" the group—there are no fees or costs associated with subscribing.

○ In the search box on the screen type in the topic you are interested in (**scuba, baseball, politics**) and a list of Newsgroups related to your topic of interest will be listed.

○ Click on the ones of interest to you to add them to your reading list.

○ Double-click one of the groups from your reading list to display the list of postings to that Newsgroup. If a *Newsgroup* is akin to an electronic bulletin board, a *posting* is the electronic equivalent of a 3" × 5" card pinned to that bulletin board.

○ Double-click on the description that interests you most from the list of postings.

The contents of that posting will be displayed for you to read.

After you have read the post, you can either read the next posting, reply to the one you have just read by selecting the **Reply** button and typing your response, save the post to a file on your computer (select the **File** pull-down menu and select **Save.** You will be prompted to save the file just as you would in any other application), or simply **Quit** Newsgroups.

Try out several different Newsgroups to get the feel for how they work. Try a trial reply to one of the postings. Simply type **test** in the reply box and send it. Come back later and you will see your reply there for the world to see. Since most of you are concerned about what your kids might get into in this area try typing **sex, erotic,** or **pictures** into the topic search area and see what comes back.

Exercise 7: IRC (Internet Relay Chat)

One final exercise while you are still on the Internet: Select the IRC icon from your main menu and let's try a chat session or two. Before we get into a chat session we will need to tell the program where to connect by setting the server address. From the pull-down menus select **IRC** or **Edit** then **Server** (see Figure 7.9) and input one of the following in the box marked **Host**.

If you have trouble connecting or get a reply that the server is full simply repeat this step and try another:

○ cs-pub.bu.edu

○ poe.acc.virginia.edu

○ irc.eskimo.com

○ irc.digex.net

○ irc-2.mit.edu

○ irc.colorado.edu

○ irc.iastate.edu

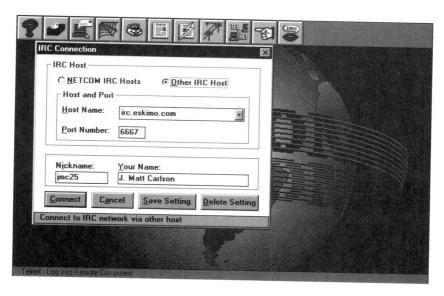

Figure 7.9 *Select the IRC icon and fill in a host name.*

Click on **Connect** and the IRC Chat Window will open (see Figure 7.10). The three parts of the window are:

○ Public area

○ Participants window

○ Input area

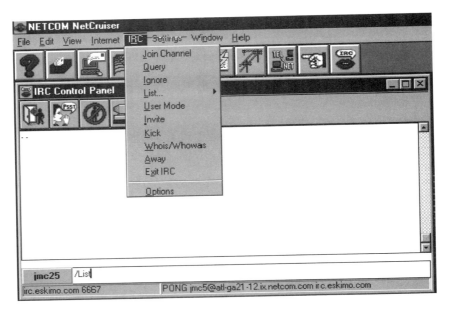

Figure 7.10 *Use icons or pull-down menus to get a list of available chat groups.*

○ Type **/list** in the Input Area and press **Return.** A list of available chat groups will scroll onto the screen. At any given time there may be as many as ten thousand chat rooms operating. Simply select one that looks interesting based on its name.

○ Double-click on the channel name to join the channel or if you know the name of a channel you wish to join, skip the list by using the icon in the menu bar to join a channel. Type the name of the channel (most of them are preceded by **#**) and click the **Join** button.

○ When the channel opens in the Public area, a list of participants will fill the right hand window (Participants window) and you will begin to see the conversation between the participants take place in the Public area. If you want to join in, just type what you want to say in the Input area and press **Return**. If no participants appear in the Participants window it is possible that you are the only one in the room. Just quit that room by closing the window (just as you would any other window) and select another from the list.

Getting Involved

Many of the solutions to inappropriate material available today are exclusionary in their approach. That is, they attempt to block out the negative. The challenge with this approach lies in the rapidity with which new material is developed, new sites become available, and the breakneck pace of changing technology. That is not to say I don't applaud and support those efforts. In fact, I believe that access control software developed for that purpose is a fundamental component of creating a childproof Internet and is one of the only real solutions available to parents of older kids.

However, I believe those efforts should be superseded with an inclusionary approach with goals of proactively identifying the material that is age appropriate, supports academic endeavors, and broadens cultural horizons, leading our children to it. For years, parents have taught their children how to avoid strangers, and instilled values that steer them away from more traditional forms of trouble. To the extent that this works in the real world, it should easily transfer into the world of the Internet.

For most of us it is easy to become involved in our kids' sports or school activities. As high-tech parents we must also learn to become involved in our kids online activities. Likewise, we must also involve our kids in what we do online. Take the time to share with them how you use the computer for work, pull email from home and show them what kind of messages you get. Begin to track your investments online and have them help by looking up the latest quotes or plotting the daily highs and lows in a spreadsheet program. Involvement with our kids is especially tough for parents of teens. Teens are getting to the point where they cherish their independence and want to try their wings. As with many other things, it will take some creativity to stay involved or at least aware of what your kids are doing online during those years. Freedom and independence doesn't mean that you have to turn the reins over completely any more than it does with the car, dating or any of the other issues parents of teens face. The possibilities for involvement with your kids are limitless. They are bounded only by the collective creativity and interests of you and your children.

It is not the intent of this section to be all-encompassing. Rather, what follows are a few suggestions of activities that not only allow you to be involved with your kids but also help to manage inappropriate material.

BUILD SETS OF WORLD WIDE WEB BOOKMARKS FOR EACH FAMILY MEMBER

Begin by sitting down together and making a list of some areas you want to explore. Make sure when you sit down in front of the computer, you have a pen and paper handy as you will want to write down the address of some of the sites you go to. I actually keep a stenographers notebook next to the computer so I can jot notes of places of interest that I stumble across.

Start with the World Wide Web (the Web). It is the easiest place to search and is filled with graphical surprises. You might want to start with Safety Net Services Homepage since it has links to virtually all of the major search engines in addition to a Kids Only page (See Appendix B).

○ Select one of these search engines (Yahoo and Webcrawler are very easy to use).

○ Type in one of your interest categories, and press **Return**.

○ If the number of responses to your search is too large, add an additional search term that will limit the responses. For instance. If you used NBA as your search term you could conceivably get thousands of responses. The search engine takes your search term and looks for any document on the Internet that has a reference to the NBA and returns that document's address as part of your search. You can imagine that could be quite a few documents. So let's suppose what we really want to see is stuff about Michael Jordan and the Chicago Bulls.

○ In the search box type the following: **Jordan AND Chicago AND Bulls AND NBA** and press **Return**. By adding additional search terms to our initial search we have reduced the number of responses. Here is why. Using our additional search terms, the Web now looks for those documents containing not only the NBA but also Jordan *and* Chicago *and* Bulls and returns a much smaller portion of the total search we did earlier.

There are a number of search "connectors" you can use. Some of the most common are:

○ **AND** Documents must include both search terms.

○ **OR** Documents returned may include either of the search terms listed (Jordan OR Bulls would get us documents that had either listing but not necessarily both).

○ **NOT** Excludes documents with the additional search term (NBA NOT Bulls would return those pages about the NBA but that nothing to do with the Bulls).

○ **ADJ** Returns documents where the search terms are adjacent to each other (Chicago ADJ Bulls would keep us from getting miscellaneous information about Chicago or bull fights in Madrid).

Try several different searches. First try one from your kids' list and then try one from yours. As you go from page to page of your searches note that each page has a separate "address" at the top. These addresses will usually start with http:// and be followed by a long string of letters and numbers. When you find a page you want to go back to, jot the address down in your log book, or create a *bookmark* in your electronic address book (I bet you didn't even know you had one). Many of the site names are long and hard to remember so most Web browsers have a feature that lets you easily set up a list of *bookmarks* referring to particular sites. Let me show you how.

Up until now, each time you wanted to use Yahoo you had to type in **http://www.yahoo.com/.** So type that into the address line on the Web once more, but before you enter a search term let's set a bookmark so we can easily get back here again. Referring to Figure 7.11, do the following:

○ Use the **WWW** or **Bookmarks** pull-down menu to access the book-mark window. The window will show the current address (in this case **http://www.yahoo.com**) and provide a space to type in a more common name that describes the site (Yahoo).

○ Click on **Add** and the name you typed in will appear in the list of bookmarks you have created.

○ To get to this site in the future, simply access the bookmark window (using the icon or pull-down menu), click on **Yahoo** and click **on JUMP**.

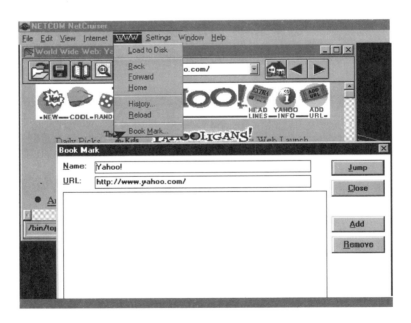

Figure 7.11 Add Bookmarks to make getting back again a snap!

As part of the agreement we talked about in Chapter 6, we discussed agreeing on appropriate sites. By setting up bookmarks for sites you have previewed and agreed upon together, you have created one way of conveniently enforcing that agreement. While this will not prevent children from accessing other areas, creating a set of bookmarks for each child is a good way to steer him or her toward more age appropriate sites.

REPLACE YOUR WEB BROWSER'S HOME PAGE WITH ONE YOU SELECT

When you begin a session on the World Wide Web, you often begin at your ISP's home page or some other pre-selected site. From there you can access other areas of the Web. Using the **Preferences** or **Settings** menu from your Web browser, you can configure it to start at a site that contains references to child-appropriate Internet site—Like Safety Net Services "Kids Only" page (see Appendix B) or another one of your choosing.

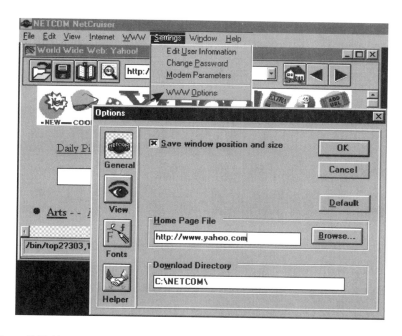

Figure 7.12 You can set your home page on the WWW to virtually anyplace you desire .

○ Click on **Settings**.

○ Click on **WWW Options**.

○ Type the **address** of your new home page in the box labeled **Home Page File**.

○ Click **OK**.

The next time you open your Web browser, it should automatically default to the new home page you selected. Again this won't prevent kids from wandering but by starting them out in places of interest and intrigue, the chances of them spending their allotted time online productively are greatly increased.

FAMILY NIGHTS

For some time now, our family has designated an evening every other week or so as a family night online. One of us is designated the leader and is responsible for setting the theme. I suggest you rotate it through the family. You will be amazed at what your kids come up with. That person will go online during the week and do the research to find sites and set bookmarks so that on Friday night when we gather around the computer, we already have a starting point to work from. Interestingly enough, I can only think of once or twice that we have ever ended the evening on the same topic we started with. Some of the topics we have used are:

- ◯ Shopping for a new car.
- ◯ Looking at colleges.
- ◯ Tracking stocks and setting up a portfolio.
- ◯ Planning a trip—looking at sites, making reservations, you can even get a map (check out **http://www.mapquest.com/**).

What others can you thinks of? One other thing we do is to order pizza in on family night. The sauce on the keyboard is a mess but it is worth it!

CREATE A SET OF CUSTOM SUBSCRIPTION SITES FOR NEWSGROUPS

In addition to Internet Access Control software (see Chapter 8) a little up-front planning can help weed out some of the hazards inherent to the Usenet Newsgroups while allowing your children to access their many benefits.

To access Newsgroups, you must *subscribe* to them—remember Exercise 6? Once you have subscribed to a Newsgroup, the name of the group appears on a *subscription list*. By previewing each site you and your child can then set up a subscription list of acceptable Newsgroups and agree that they will only visit those sites. You should then periodically check to make sure undesirable sites have not been added to the list by your child. One final step would be to add such a list to a home page of your own creation that would reflect both bookmarks and subscription sites as links that are available at the click of a mouse.

BUILD YOUR OWN HOME PAGE

Here is the ultimate thrill. Surfing the Internet may be fun, but building your own site is even more so. Many newbies don't realize how easy it is to build and browse their own home page. Best of all, there are many excellent free and shareware tools (such as Microsoft's Internet Assistant, HTML Web Weaver, etc.) available for generating home pages. Instead of spending hours looking at other sites, your children could be spending time building their own sites and learning programming skills!

It is clearly beyond the scope of this book to teach you how to build a home page and there are many other sources (many of them free online, try doing a Webcrawler search) far better than me to learn from.

But let me suggest a couple of places to start:

http://www. ncsa.uiuc.edu/General/Internet/WWW/HTMLPrimer.html
http://members.aol.com/htmlguru/about_html.html

These are both good starting spots that provide lots of descriptions and step by step instructions about how to start building a homepage.

http://www.cc.ukans.edu/info/HTML_quick.html

This site is a glossary of HTML commands and I would recommend printing it out so you can keep it handy as you start to write your own pages

Your homepage can be created in any word processing program but when you save the file be sure to save it as a text-only file and add an .html or .htm extension to the file name. For example, safesurf.htm where ".htm" is the file extension. This allows your browser to recognize the file as a web document.

One final hint...

The HTML file for home pages that already exist can be easily viewed from within your browser. Just select a homepage you like the looks of and click Source from the View menu. The HTML file that creates the web page you are looking at will be displayed.

This little trick allows you to see how the experts code their files and there is nothing to stop you from copying their styles for your own home page. To use these files either print the document after you have used the View-Source command or use Edit-Select All and copy the text into your word processor. Once you have modified it with your name and information you will have a pretty neat homepage.

For inspiration, check out Kids Club at **http://huizen.dds.nl:80/~ink,** run by Jonathan Puckey, a 14-year-old Brit who resides in Holland. Make building your own Home Page one of your first family nights and I think you will be surprised at how much fun and just how easy it can be.

Way to go! You are no longer a newbie. I know you aren't quite ready for your propeller beanie yet and that most of these tasks felt really awkward. That's OK, don't let it deter you from doing them enough that you get comfortable. The best advice I can give you is to take your time. Realize that families are just beginning to use this tool and that makes you a pioneer. And while pioneers were always ahead of the pack and often got the gold they also got the most arrows. If you get stuck, ask your kids for help. If they can't help, you can always go to the pull-down menus and simply exit the program. This will end the task you are doing and you can just log on again. Finally, remember that you *can* be an Internet expert (or at least appear to be one), you *can* keep up with your kids and by the time you are done with this book, you *will* know more than most other people out there.

What to Do When You Aren't Home

Access Control Software

The best way for parents to make online time safe and friendly is to be involved but let's get real. Even if our kids wanted us around 24 hours a day, seven days a week, jobs and other commitments would still draw us away. Two income families are more prevalent than ever, drawing parents even further from kids. Kids are also demanding and all too often getting increased freedom at much younger ages than most of us ever did. We just can't always be there when our kids are online.

Access Control Software gives parents the tools they need to shield children from inappropriate material when they can't be there. Blocking 100% of the objectionable material is an impossible task. New Web sites are being set up daily, new servers can be attached to the Internet at any time, and IRC chat rooms and Newsgroups are dynamic by their very nature. Don't let that stop you from including the most advanced technological solutions available as part of your response to this challenge. These filters don't claim to block 100%, but they do an admirable job, even when you can't be there.

In this chapter, we will not only discuss how these products work but also review some of the most popular ones available today. An understanding of how each works will assist you not only in making a decision about which to purchase but also make you aware of its limitations. In that way you can manage the environment in which it is used so you don't place undue reliance on the software and in doing so create a liability rather than a solution.

How Access Control Software Works

Though each program takes a little different approach, the basic premise is the same. The software creates a "filter" through which the information coming into your machine must pass. This filter consists of one or more databases which contain the "addresses" of sites known to be objectionable and by comparing the incoming data to that list, the programs either allows it to pass through or blocks access and notifies the user. The more advanced programs also create a second filter based on words (sex, bomb, nazi, porno, ass, breast, etc.) or letter combinations (sado, uck, gasm, etc.). This second filter becomes very important because of the dynamic nature of the Internet. New servers, Web sites, Newsgroups, and Chat groups are created every day (if not quicker). Depending on how diligent the researchers compiling the list are, it may be several days or longer until a site is evaluated and added to the database or until parents download the list to their computer. These "dictionaries" of unacceptable words and letter groups essentially form a backdrop to prevent otherwise unacceptable material from slipping through. This method is surprisingly effective and repeatedly caught sites in our tests that would have otherwise been available. High-end products also offer one or both of two additional means of control—time restrictions and restrictions from running programs that are resident on the computer but have nothing to do with the Internet. AOL, Prodigy, Quicken or games programs might fall into this category. Using a routine similar to the site filter, the program compares the time of day a user is requesting access as well as the particular program for which they are requesting access. If either of these violates predetermined restrictions, the program creates a warning and restricts access. In some programs it goes as far as to lock access to the program until the administrator (you in most cases) resets the alarm. In this way you are aware that a violation has taken place.

Choosing an Access Control Program

To determine what program best suits your needs first answer the following questions:

○ Do you want the program to operate with or without your children's knowledge?

○ Do you want the program to enforce time restrictions?

○ Do you want to build the database of sites and words or do you want someone else to do it for you?

○ Do you want the program to control access to other parts of your computer other than the Internet?

OVERT OR COVERT?

Two very distinct types of blocking software are available today. The first operates in what can be called a "stealth" or covert mode. These programs are transparent to the user but create a log of any violations that take place. Parents can examine the log to determine if their kids have been living up to their agreement. Parents also have the option of creating a block to objectionable sites as well but obviously this would render the "stealth" aspect unusable.

The second type of product operates in a "cooperative" mode. Parents are encouraged to sit down with their children and cooperatively set operating parameters. This mode gives parents a chance to discuss with their kids what is appropriate and why and no one is surprised by their inability to later access those areas that are off limits.

OTHER CONSIDERATIONS

For the purpose of selecting the "best" access control software, I answered yes to the remainder of the questions so that our selection would reflect the broadest level of protection. However only you can decide how you want to raise your children and what experiences are appropriate for them. Every family is unique and different experiences are appropriate in different families. For that reason an effective access control program must respond to these varying needs and be robust enough to block the materials, yet be flexible enough to allow for individual needs. Only one of the products we looked at adequately responded to all these requirements—CyberPatrol. I have provided the review of CyberPatrol followed by a table that compares the features of CyberPatrol to the other access control products we tested. Reviews of these products then make up the balance of the chapter.

Table 8.1 A Comparison of Access Control Software

	Cyber Patrol	CYBERsitter	Surf Watch	Net Nanny
Company	Microsystems Software	Solid Oak Software	SurfWatch Software	Net Nanny
Platforms	Windows 3.1 Windows95 Mac OS	Windows 3.1 Windows95	Windows 3.1 Windows95 Mac OS	Windows 3.1 DOS
Internet Address	http://www.microsys.com	http://www.solidoak.com	http://www.surfwatch.com	http://www.netnanny.com
Downloadable	Yes	Yes	Demo	Yes
Price	$35.00[1] Includes 6 months of updates	$39.95 Updates are free	$49.95 Includes two months of updates	$49.95 No updates available
Update Costs	$19.95/ 6 months	Free	$6.00/ month	Not Available
Blocks JPEG & GIF	Yes	Yes	Yes	Yes
Blocks Binary Downloads	Yes	Yes	No	Yes
Blocks Gopher & FTP	Yes	No	Yes	Yes
Blocks IRC	Yes	Yes	Yes	Yes
Blocks ZIP and SIT Transfers	Yes	Yes	No	Yes
Blocks Newsgroups	Yes	Yes	Yes	Yes
Blocks Transmission of Personal Information	Yes	Yes	No	Yes
Blocks Offensive Language	Yes	Yes	No	Yes
Blocks User Programs	Yes	No	No	Yes
Works w/ Commercial Providers	All	AOL, CompuServe, Prodigy	None	All
Enforces Time Limits	Yes	No	No	No
User Definable Data Base	Yes	No	No	Yes

[1]Ordered directly from Safety Net Services. Retail Price is $49.95 if downloaded or purchased from Microsystems Software

Testing the Traps

All of the packages that we reviewed do a good job of preventing access to inappropriate material. To accomplish this task, each package takes a somewhat different approach. Some of them provide lists of inappropriate sites and most of those programs provide online updates, but these differ in cost and regularity. Some of the programs allow the user to also block key words, while others allow the user to block execution of certain programs. These programs are sure to evolve over time, and as the nature of the threat of the "dark side" of the Internet changes, so too will the features found in the blocking software.

In addition to testing the program according to the manufacturers directions, our testing included numerous attempts to disable the software. To test each program we erased all evidence of the program in configuration files, deleted it from the Startup program group, deleted all files that we found that appeared to be related to the program (including their hidden files), and generally tried to destroy it. With the exception of one, all continued to operate. While this does not mean that it would be impossible for a crafty and very talented hacker to disable the programs, they would have to spend a substantial amount of time doing so and would be more likely to disable the boot sector of their computer than bypass the software. In fact, twice we were forced to reformat our hard drives as a result of our efforts.

CyberPatrol

For total features, ability to customize and availability/completeness of updates, CyberPatrol is the best choice currently available for parents wishing to police their kids' use of the Internet. CyberPatrol is the most comprehensive of all of the programs tested with controls for specific sites, specific word, and letter groupings, time limitations and controls for non-Internet games and applications. The heart of the program is the "CyberNOT" list, a customizable filtering dictionary that can be updated online on a weekly basis. This is the most frequent update available from any program.

We were especially impressed with CyberPatrol's time limitation tools, accessed from the password-protected "Headquarters." All configuration of the program takes place from the Headquarters. Here parents can not only adjust the hours of use by day of the week but also by total hours per day and hours per week. For example, you can turn Internet access off during school and homework hours, allow a few hours of access in the evening and then block access from 10:00 p.m. until the next morning. This is also where parents can deny access to IRC channels, Newsgroups, the WWW, or FTP sites as well as customize the list of inappropriate sites and words—the CyberNOT list.

The CyberNOT list is broken up into twelve categories that allow parents the flexibility to enforce restrictions based on their own moral values. Parents can also deny access to sites not included on the list by simply adding them from the Configure Settings menu. The list can be updated online weekly and will only add new sites so it won't erase any customization you may have done to the list. A six month subscription to the list is included with the software and an additional six-month subscription costs $19.95. Think of it as a low-cost insurance policy that creates a cyber-safe environment for your children.

CyberPatrol also allows a parent to block access to non-Internet programs. A parent can block access to up to eight programs allowing restricted access to games or programs that initiate online services like America Online or CompuServe.

Pros

- ○ Very comprehensive methods used to block access.
- ○ Time blocking features.
- ○ Provides blocking for online services like CompuServe, AOL, and Prodigy.
- ○ Windows 3.x, Windows 95, and Macintosh versions available.
- ○ If program detects tampering, it totally shuts down Internet access until you contact tech support.

Cons

○ $19.95 per six months to update CyberNOT list.

○ Program is visible when in use—no stealth operation.

INSTALLING THE PROGRAM

CyberPatrol installs easily in a matter of minutes. The program uses a password system to allow access to CyberPatrol's Headquarters (the main control panel where a parent sets up the security scheme). The Headquarters password gives full access to Headquarters, while the Deputy password gives temporary, but full access to all Internet services. The Deputy password is only good through the end of the day it is assigned and is ideal for assigning extra time or unrestricting access to do research in otherwise restricted areas.

To install the program simply insert the disk into the A:Drive and type **a:cp-setup**. At the setup screen click **OK** to install the program to the CyberPatrol directory and the program will complete the installation. CyberPatrol will place the program in your computer's Startup folder so the program will launch each time you turn on your computer and place an icon in the top left corner of your Program Manager screen (or task bar for Windows 95 users).

To configure the program, double-click the **yellow badge** icon and you will be prompted to enter a password. Carefully type in a password you will remember and click the **Validate Password** button. The next screen is CyberPatrol's Headquarters. It is from this screen that you make any changes to the programs configuration and save those changes (see Figure 8.1).

To change the time restrictions, click the **Set Hours of Operation** button **click** on the particular half-hour you wish to turn on or off. The block will turn either red (off) or green (on) indicating its current status. You may also set the total number of hours allowed each day as well as the total allowed each week. This allows your children to learn to budget their time online without you having to be there or remind them of their limits.

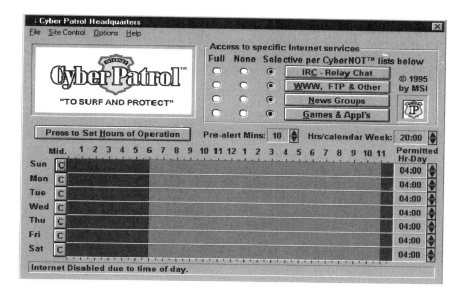

Figure 8.1 CyberPatrol's Headquarters screen.

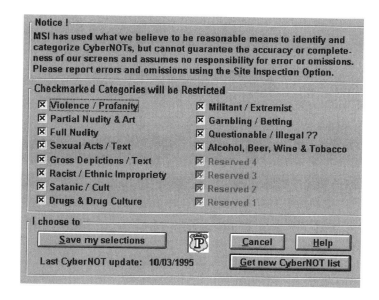

Figure 8.2 CyberPatrol's Category Restriction menu.

To customize the site restrictions or update the CyberNOT list, click the **Site Control** menu and select **Category Restrictions** (see Figure 8.2).

Turn each category on or off by clicking the box to its left. If you are online you can update the CyberNOT list by simply clicking the "Get New CyberNOT List" button.

CYBERsitter

The distinguishing feature of CYBERsitter is its ability to run in "stealth mode." This means that the user does not know that the program is running in the background. Unlike the other programs that we reviewed, this means that you can monitor a child's activity without them knowing that they are being monitored. Access to inappropriate material is then recorded in a password-accessible database so you can review your child's activity. In addition to the stealth mode, CYBERsitter can also be configured to block access and to both report and block. You can even keep a running log of all Internet sites that a particular user visits.

CYBERsitter blocks access based on a list of words, phrases, and letter groupings within Web, FTP sites, and Newsgroups. It operates on three levels: it blocks access to specific Internet resources, it censors specific words, and it acts as a filter for different file types, applications, or documents. CYBERsitter's list is updated frequently and updates are available free of charge online. Users can also enter their phone number and address, and if the program detects that that information is about to be sent over the Internet, the transmission is blocked. This is a great feature. It is designed to keep your children from giving out their phone number or address. However, a particularly disappointing aspect of the program is the inability to directly customize CYBERsitter's list of unacceptable sites by adding or excluding certain sites. However, the program does make provisions to send an email to CYBERsitter's developers with a word and or site, and presumably they will add it to their list after it has been researched. CYBERsitter's web site is **http://www.rain.org/~solidoak/cybersit.htm**.

CYBERsitter was easy to install and like the other programs, access to the controls portion of the program is controlled by a password.

One disappointing feature was that the program was too easy to disable. By removing a single command in one of the configuration files, CYBERsitter was effectively removed after rebooting the computer. The developers of the program recognize this and have given you the ability to prohibit access to these configuration files. However, there are valid reasons a user might need to access these files, and locking them out can keep a user from using the computer for valid purposes.

Overall, CYBERsitter is a good program for blocking inappropriate access to the Internet. It really shines when it comes to its stealth mode and its free site list upgrades.

PROS

○ Runs in a stealth mode allowing you to monitor your children's use without their knowledge.

○ Free site and inappropriate-word updates.

○ Blocks transmission of your home address or telephone numbers.

○ Allows you to block access to an unlimited number of files.

○ Works with CompuServe, America Online and Prodigy.

CONS

○ Windows version only, no Macintosh or Windows 95 version available.

○ To prevent the program to be disabled, you will have prohibit access to Windows configuration files or menu items.

○ No time limit limitations.

SurfWatch

SurfWatch was the first of the blocking programs to be released. Unfortunately, it is already showing its age. While easy to install, parents cannot customize the database, nor is the 2000 site database anywhere near as complete as CyberPatrol's 7500 entry database. No monitoring or reporting capabilities are available either. SurfWatch's Web site is **http://www.surfwatch.com**.

SurfWatch installs easily in a few minutes. You can then go immediately online and update its database of offensive sites, though we consistently received an error when trying to update the site database. The program is automatically loaded when the computer is booted and the program can only be enabled and disabled if you have the password.

PROS

○ Very easy to install and configure.

○ Windows 3.1, Windows 95 and Macintosh versions available.

CONS

○ Uses a proprietary site list to which the user does not have access.

○ No time restriction control.

○ No way for the user to update the list without subscribing to SurfWatch's update maintenance plan.

○ The maintenance plan costs around $6.00 per month, making it the most expensive program to keep updated.

○ Cannot be used with America Online, CompuServe, or Prodigy.

○ Lacks reporting or monitoring capabilities.

○ No stealth mode or activity logging.

Net Nanny

Net Nanny's distinguishing feature is its ability to function as a total security program for your computer. Net Nanny constantly monitors all activity for the use of keywords, phrases, or other information stored in its user definable dictionary regardless of whether that activity is on the Internet or not. If a violation occurs the computer will either "blank" the screen, shut down the offending application, or shut down the entire system depending on how the program has been configured. Net Nanny's Web site is **http://www.netnanny.com/netnanny/**.

Because Net Nanny can be configured to block both outgoing as well as incoming communications, parents can use the dictionary to keep information like their address, phone numbers and credit card data from being transmitted without their knowledge.

Although Net Nanny's technique is intriguing, its implementation is awkward. Setup requires parents to load words, phrases and specific sites into Net Nanny's dictionary manually which is very time-consuming. This premise also necessitates staying one step ahead of your children by constantly adding new sites.

Use of the program makes your system noticeably slower and any changes to the program require the original installation disk, making administration a headache.

One last negative about the program is its DOS-based install and setup. The easy access to configuration files and manipulation of the program made bypassing Net Nanny a snap for even the least accomplished hacker.

PROS

○ Blocks incoming and outgoing communications.

○ Works for both Internet and non-Internet applications providing total computer security.

CONS

○ Cumbersome setup and maintenance without downloadable list or dictionary.

○ No site updates.

○ Slows computer processing noticeably.

○ Easily by-passed or corrupted.

○ No Windows 95 or Macintosh version.

Just a Couple More Things

As we wind down there are just a couple more things I want to mention that didn't seem to fit any place else in the book—so they go here. After you read these suggestions you might sit back and say, everybody knows that, and you are probably right.

What and Where are Important, Too

Throughout the book we have focused on a number of things that can be very time-consuming, but trust me when I tell you they are worth every minute. But some of the simplest things can also pay big dividends. I often refer to this section of my seminar as "working the scene of the crime." Using simple techniques you can often cut off problems before they happen—or at least pick up on the clues that a problem exists.

The single most effective action you will take as a parent to control the computer is to put it in a common place. Many times computers become hand-me-downs. Parents purchase newer, faster machines and give the old machine to the kids. What happens next is that machine finds its way into the child's room or down into the basement. When the computer is that far away, I can assure you that you have no idea what it is being used for. You will have much better control over who, what, and when if the computer is sitting in the family room. What are the chances of Johnny downloading naked pictures while you are reading the newspaper, cooking, or sewing in the next room?

Next I would encourage you to look for fingerprints, not on the keyboard but on your hard drive. Saving pictures on the computer is a very memory-intensive process (whether they are good or bad pictures doesn't matter). In order to transmit these documents both economically and quickly, those uploading the files will usually use a compression program to reduce the size of the file. These compression programs add what is called a file extension to the end of the file name to tell you what kind of decoder you need to uncompress the file on the other end. The four most common compression schemes are **.jpg**, **.gif**, **uue**, and **zip**. When you download one of these files your computer will decompress the file and save it on your hard drive, usually to the download directory in your service providers folder. That is where you go into action. Open either **the File Manager** (IBM) or **Hard Drive** (Mac) folder from the desktop and select **Search** (IBM) or **Find** (Mac) from the File pull-down menu. In the Search box, type the following: ***.jpg** (just **jpg** on the Mac) and press **Return**. Repeat the process using **gif**, **zip**, and **uue** in place of **jpg**. In each case, your computer will search its memory for any file that has that file extension and display a list. Scan the names of the files and determine if there are any of suspicious character. If you have recently been on a "Cyber safari" having files named *chetah.jpg* shouldn't disturb you much but if you begin to find files with names like *suzi&chetah.jpg* you may want to look further. You can generally look at these files by double-clicking on them. The viewer configured for your computer will then load the particular file and display the photograph on the screen. That is not to say that if no such files exist on your hard drive you are home free. It doesn't take a very accomplished criminal to wipe the fingerprints off a smoking gun. To delete these files from your computer, just click on the file and from the File menu select **Delete**. More importantly, sit down and have a candid (and probably difficult) conversation with your child about your agreement, what's appropriate for them, and what the consequences of the violation are.

Two other tell-tale signs to look for are a marked slowdown in the speed of your machine and reduced available hard drive space. Remember, picture files require a lot of memory and when they are saved to your hard drive in quantity you will notice these symptoms. Again, search for and delete all the files that are not necessary. Not all graphic files are bad, and if you find ones you want to save during your search simply save them to a disk for future use. Don't forget to label the disk or you will find yourself searching through dozens of unlabeled disks some-day in the future when you can least afford the time.

Computer Got a Cold?

After all, a cold is just a virus. But the kind of virus we are talking about is really more like a cancer than a cold, and while contracting one from being online is rare, it pays to take precautions.

A *virus* is a rogue computer software program created to infect other programs with copies of itself. Most of these programs are relatively harmless and mildly amusing when they make your computer start to sing or blink or some other childish prank. However, some are written to dam-age programs and data. Worst of all is that you or I have no idea which one does what.

In the past, viruses were spread through the exchange of floppy disks "infected" with the virus. Now, the advent of networks and online services has created a whole new, and imminently more dangerous, environment for the spread of viruses. Exchanging files on a network or downloading files from an FTP site or bulletin board can easily cause your computer to become infected. To protect your computer from these potentially hazardous invaders is relatively easy if you take some simple precautions.

First, install an antiviral software product. These products can be configured to screen any program being loaded to your machine for viruses and when one is detected, to eliminate it. A particularly good one is VirusScan95 from McAfee Associates. You can obtain an evaluation copy online from their Web site at **http://www.mcafee.com**. They make downloading as simple as a click of the mouse, and the program is self-installing so you don't have to worry about that either. You do have to worry about sending them a check if you decide to keep the product.

Use the scanning software. Viruses are a bit like "undesirable" material on the Internet. Just when you think you have taken care of it, new sites pop up. To prevent viruses from infecting your computer will take some diligence on your part to assist the antivirus program. You must update your software periodically to add any newly discovered or created viruses to the program's memory. The software essentially scans your memory (hard drives, floppy disks when they are inserted, or network drives) looking for the "signatures" of known viruses. Set up a monthly routine to update the software online and then scan your hard drive.

Back up all critical data and programs. That way, if you have a problem you will only have bad or corrupted data back to the point of your last backup.

Avoid downloading files to your hard disk. Use a floppy instead and then re-insert the floppy to load the program. Most virus programs are configured to check all floppy disks when they are inserted, as this has been the most common way of spreading viruses in the past.

Resist the temptation to use pirated software. This has been a known source of viruses for years and is easily avoided. Again, make sure you scan any disks you insert into your machine to be sure they are "clean."

A Special Place for Everyone

One last thought on using your hardware to create a safe environment is that of creating a "room" for each of your children on the computer. There are a number of software products that allow you to individualize access to the various parts of the computer by setting up individual "desktops." These programs will automatically start up with Windows and are password-protected, so each child will have his or her own password to get into their room. When parents install the program the first time, they create a master password, which is used to create and modify each room, so don't forget the password you choose. When creating a room you can select what programs are available to the child, you can restrict access to areas (like your financial programs or maybe even the Internet access program), and leave other areas completely unprotected. These programs are very flexible and are especially good with younger children. One such program that is very inexpensive (approximately $25), is KidDesk Family Edition from Edmark Corp. Edmark is the maker of a number of great kids' programs that pepper our software library, and this is just an extension of an already great product line. Unfortunately, they do not have a version for Macintosh yet, but if you are a Windows 3.x or Windows 95 user and you have young kids you may want to check this out.

Closing Thoughts

In an environment where parents are increasingly prone to shift their responsibility to schools, governments, or even neighbors, we have deliberately taken a different tack. We have talked about parents getting involved with their kids, especially as it relates to technology. If we remain ignorant to the dangers of technology, our kids will find their way into trouble there just as surely as they would if left to roam at the mall or through the neighborhood unsupervised. We have introduced you to a hierarchical approach that should help you determine what types of involvement are most appropriate. At the same time, we have shown you how to use the technology so that you won't be completely unfamiliar when you sit down for the first time in front of your machine. Finally, we have introduced you to some tools that will fill your shoes when you can't be there. But there are risks and limitations to each of these approaches because they are just tools, not miracle cures. It is easy to get a little training or install blocking software and lull yourself into a false sense of security. After all, you are informed, right? In the year since we began Safety Net Services, technology has changed many times, and it will continue to do so. With each change comes new challenges. The world of technology simply isn't one where you can set the autopilot and go to sleep. It will take perseverance and diligence to stay ahead—or to just keep up. A tool in the hands of a craftsman really does appear to do miraculous things, but that same tool in the hands of an amateur can be very dangerous. So it is with the tools we have introduced in this book. The only commonality all the approaches we have presented in this book have is *you*. You can make a difference for your kids, for my kids, and for many others just like them, but you have to get involved. I assure you I will be down at the seashore tomorrow, and the next day and the next, making a difference, one life at a time. Won't you join me?

Safety Net Checklist

This list is meant to serve as a desktop companion to assist you in creating a cybersafe environment. Simply work through each category, placing a checkmark next to those items that you do. When you get to the end, you will have gone a long way toward creating the kind of technological environment you can feel good about.

Where Are Your Kids?

Look at the diagram below and based on your child's age and skill level determine what actions may be appropriate.

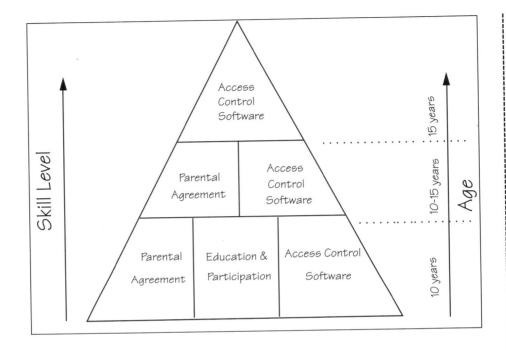

Where Are You?

Put a check in the box if you know what the right answer is. Use the glossary to find out.

❏ Computer: ❏ IBM   ❏ Mac

❏ Modem

❏ Windows: ❏ 3.1   ❏ Win95

❏ Internet Service Provider (ISP)

❏ Commercial Service Provider

❏ World Wide Web

❐ Netiquette

❐ Chat Group

❐ Newsgroup

Hardware Configuration

In order to set up your Internet connection you will need to know the following:

❐ IBM: ❐ 386   ❐ 486   ❐ Pentium

❐ Macintosh: ❐ 68030   ❐ 69040   ❐ Power Mac

❐ Operating System: ❐ Window 3.x   ❐ Windows 95
    ❐ Mac System 7x

❐ Modem Speed: ❐ 9600 bps   ❐ 14.4 Kbps ❐ 28.8 Kbps

Selecting a Service Provider

❐ How many kids? _____

❐ Hours Needed_____(Kids x 10 to get *minimum* number of hours/month online)

❐ Commercial Provider *or* ISP (What special services of a commercial provider would you use? If none, choose ISP.)

❐ Cost   ❐ Flat rate/ unlimited usage
    ❐ Base rate *plus* hourly usage fees

❏ Local access number ( ) ___-____

❏ Modem Speeds Supported _____
(Faster = less time online = less $$)

❏ Parental Controls Available

❏ Test Drive or free hours first month

Create an Agreement

What terms belong in your agreement?

❏ Time Limits   <u>S</u>   <u>M</u>   <u>T</u>   <u>W</u>   <u>T</u>   <u>F</u>   <u>S</u>
(hours)   ____ ____ ____ ____ ____ ____ ____

❏ How many hours per week? _____   Per month? _____

❏ Information not to disseminate

❏ Appropriate places to go (Check the sites out together)

❏ Appropriate uses   % Study_____   % Play_____

❏ Budget limits $_____

❏ Value Added (point system, allowance contribution, etc)

❏ Netiquette

❏ What to do in unpleasant situations

❏ Meeting people in person that you met online

❏ Rules of Conduct

❏ Consequences

Logistics

- ❐ Computer in common place
- ❐ Accounts set up for each person
- ❐ Online rules posted
- ❐ List of "approved" sites
- ❐ Access Control software installed

Selecting and Installing Access Control Software

- ❐ Time limits set?
- ❐ Dictionary configured   Update on:_____
- ❐ Site list configured   Update on:_____
- ❐ Block additional sites or programs

Getting Involved

- ❐ Sites previewed / Bookmarks set
- ❐ Chat channels previewed for appropriateness
- ❐ Time together online   Date/Time _____
- ❐ Planned activities

_____

_____

Map of Safety Net's Homepage

At Safety Net, Service's, Inc. we strive to be *the* source of information about parenting and the Internet. That is not to say that we are the only people who know about the subject, just that we want to bring all those resources together for you. Our home page will give you extensive links to the information you need to make your home a CyberSafe environment. Figure B.1 is a map of what you will find.

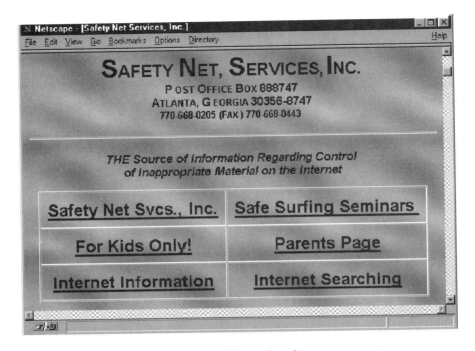

Figure B.1 http://www.safesurfing.com

Safety Net Services, Inc.

Backgrounds on the Safe Surfing team as well as reviews of the latest Internet access software and late breaking news in the world of parenting and the Internet.

For Kids Only!

Hey kids this is the place to come for the newest and best links to areas just for you on the Net! Links to Science & Math, Sports, Toys, Museums, Fun and Games, Pen Pals, International Sites, Video Games and Misc. Other Kids Sites are added frequently to give you a great place to start. You might even want to set this page up as your default home page. We will also place additional activities you can do with your kids in a special "For the Family" section.

Internet Information

Don't buy a book, check here first! Links to numerous information sources online. Many of these are FAQs but there are also extensive links to general information pages about the Internet.

Safe Surfing Seminars

A listing of upcoming seminars we will be conducting. If you are interested in learning more about how to create a childproof Internet, join us at one in your area.

Parents' Page

A place for parents to get information on the things that concern them. Links to numerous parenting sources on the Web are included here. Topics change frequently so check it out.

Internet Searching

Links to all of the most popular Internet search tools. Start here and then set bookmarks for yourself.

FAQs, Web Sites, and Other Sources of Information

FAQs

FAQs (pronounced facks) or Frequently Asked Questions lists are a great source of information once you are on the Internet. They normally have a file extension (the part after the **.**) of **.faq** and can be located using any one of the many search engines on the Web. Go ahead, try out one of the ones below.

- ○ **Internet Services FAQ** http://www.cis.ohio-state.edu/hypertext/faq/usenet/internet-services/faq/faq.html

- ○ **Internet Relay Chat (IRC)** http://www.kei.com/irc.html

- ○ **Complete listing of Usenet FAQs** http://www.cis.ohio-state.edu/hypertext/faq/usenet/

◯ **FAQs (Frequently Asked Questions)** http://www.ssrc.hku.hk/cult/faqs.html

Web Sites

There are a number of useful sites on the web for parents who are looking for information. Use a search engine using the words **Parents and Kids** and you will come with more than you will ever want. A few of my favorites are below:

Educational Resources for Parents http://execpc.com/~dboals/parents.html

Resources on Parenting & Internet Filtering http://www.pacificrim.net/~mckenzie/mar96/resource.html

Keeping Kids Safe in Cyberspace http://www.rain.org/ ~soli-doak/cyberspc.htm

Child Safety on the Information Highway http://www.omix.com/magid/child.safety.html

The National Parenting Center http://www.tnpc.com/

The CyberMom Dot Com http://www.TheCyberMom.com/

WinonaNet: Family: Parents' links http://www.luminet.net/winnet/family/parlinks.html

Parenting Resource Center on the Web http://www.parentsplace.com/

Parents and Children Together Online http://www.indiana.edu/~eric_rec/fl/pcto/menu.html

SPECTRUM: The Family Internet Magazine http://www.autobaun.com/~kbshaw/Spectrum.html

Books, Pamphlets, and Videos

America's Children & The Information Highway: A Briefing Book and National Action Agenda. 1994. Santa Monica, CA: Children's Partnership.

A Parent's Guide to the ABC's of Learning on a Home Computer. 1994. Warren Buckleitner. Cupertino, CA: Apple Computer.

Child Safety on the Information Highway. 1994. Lawrence Magid. National Center for Missing and Exploited Children, Interactive Services Association.

Internet for Kids. 1995. Ted Pedersen and Francis Moss. Price Stern Sloan.

Introduction to Internet. 1994. Digital Data Express. (70 minute videotape on how to access the Internet.)

Parents Guide to Online Fun and Learning for Kids. 1993. Edmark Corporation.

Primer of Kid-Safe
Sites Online

There are many outstanding World Wide Web sites with links to child-oriented home pages, safe newsgroups and other useful Internet sites. The "Kids Only" section of our home page at **http://www.mindspring. com/~safesurf/safesurf.html** has numerous links to many popular children's sites. Here are some of the best:

General Kid's Links

- **CyberKids http://www.cyberkids.com** An online magazine for kids by kids with stories, artwork, puzzles, links and more. Children can leave messages for each other in CyberKids Interactive.

- **The Children Page http://www.pd.astro.it/local-cgi-bin/ kids.cgi/forms** World-spanning list from Italy with an international flavor.

- **Kids http://www.gov.nb.ca/hotlist/kids.htm** Another extensive set of links to children's sites.

- **Kids Club http://huizen.dds.nl:80/~ink/**

- **Kids List http://www.clark.net/pub/journalism/kid.html**

- **The Kids on the Web http://www.zen.org/~brendan/kids.html** Dozens of links for kids (and some for parents) with descriptions.

- **Kid's Web http://www.primenet.com/~sburr/index.html**

- **Uncle Bob's Kids Page http://gagme.wwa.com/~boba/kids.html** Uncle Bob, aka Bob Allison, is one of the most prolific "linkmeisters" on the Web. This contains direct links to nearly 200 other pages.

- **Yahooligans http://www.yahooligans.com/** A subset of the famous Yahoo search engine with links to hundreds of great sites.

(These sites were current when this book was printed. Sites can change frequently. Remember that site addresses are case specific.)

For Kids Under 10

- **Kid's Corner** http://www.ot.com:80/kids/home.html

- **Theodore Tugboat** http://www.cochran.com/TT.htm

- **The Muppets Home Page** http://www.ncsa.uiuc.edu/VR/BS/ Muppets/muppets.html

○ **Dinosaurs On Line http://www.dinosauria.com/** Photos, drawings, information, and searchable links to the Pre-Cambrian Age, or was it the Jurassic?

○ **Disney http://www.disney.com/** Mickey, Goofy, and the crowd are there to help you create your own "Magic Kingdom."

Figure D.1 http://www.cyberkids.com

For Kids 10 to 15

○ **FishNet http://www.jayi.com/jayi/** Especially for teenagers.

○ **Midlink Magazine for Kids 10 to 15 http://longwood.cs. ucf.edu/~MidLink/** A wealth of geography, interesting questions, and thought-provokers. Nice site for a summer project.

○ **Children's Literature Web Guide http://www.ucalgary.ca/~ dkbrown/index.html** A sophisticated library of children's literature, including books by kids.

○ **Kids on Campus http://www.tc.cornell.edu/Kids.on.Campus/ KOC94/koc94home.html**

○ **The Great White Shark Exhibit http://ucmp1.berkeley.edu/ Doug/shark.html**

○ **Global Show-N-Tell http://emma.manymedia.com/show-n-tell/**

○ **Dinosaurs http://www.hcc.hawaii.edu/dinos/dinos.1.html**

○ **Trex via Hawaii Puzzles http://alpha.acast.nova.edu/puzzles .html** Puzzles and brain teasers from the newsgroup rec.puzzles. Solutions are provided.

○ **VidKids http://cmp1.ucr.edu/exhibitions/cmp_ed_prog.html** California Museum of Photography's Web page with an Interactive Gallery, Media Literacy Program, and Lesson Plans for Internet-savvy teachers.

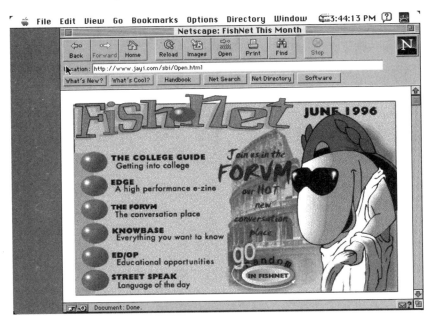

Figure D.2 http//www.Jayi.com/sbi/open.html

Games, Fun, and Fads

○ **Nintendo** http://www.nintendo.com/low/low.html

○ **Sega** http://www.segaoa.com/new/segahome.html

○ **Star Trek** http://gagme.wwa.com/~boba/trek.html Bob Allison's own Trek collection.

○ **Star Wars Home Page** http://stwing.resnet.upenn.edu:8001/~jruspini/starwars.html

○ **United Federation of Planets** http://www.imall.com/startrek/ufp.html

Chat: What Kids Want Most

Kids like chat lines because everything happens so fast. There's never a wait for a file to download, or a picture to appear. In many ways, chat is exactly what parents and teachers want kids to do: use their imaginations, instead of being force-fed images from TV, music, or movies.

○ **news:alt.kids-talk** A place for the pre-college set on the Internet.

○ **alt.support.diabetes.kids**. Support for kids with diabetes and their families.

○ **k12.chat.elementary.news:k12.chat.elementary** Talk group for elementary-school age.

○ **k12.chat.junior.news:k12.chat.junior** Talk group for junior high/middle school age.

○ **k12.chat.senior.news:k12.chat.senior** Talk group for high school age.

Other Fun Things to Do

SPORTS

○ **The Michael Jordan Page http://gagme.wwa.com/~boba/mj.html** Michael, the Bulls, NBA teams, and schedules.

○ **ESPNET SportsZone http://espnet.sportszone.com/**

FUN AND GAMES

○ **The Sugar Bush http://intranet.on.ca:80/~dlemire/sb_kids.html** Games, arts & Crafts and other fun things to do online.

○ **Games Kids Play http://www.corpcomm.net/~gnieboer/game-home.htm**

○ **Looney Tune Home Page http://www.usyd.edu.au/~swishart/looney.html**

○ **Adventure Online http://adventureonline.com**

○ **Sony http://music.sony.com**

MUSEUMS

○ **Canadian Museum of Civilization Children's Museum http://www.cmcc.muse.digital.ca/cmc/cmceng/childeng.html**

○ **Franklin Institute Virtual Science Museum http://sln.fi.edu/** They bring the exhibits, resources, and fun of a museum visit right to your desktop with virtual exhibits and hotlists.

○ **VidKids http://cmp1.ucr.edu/exhibitions/cmp_ed_prog.html** California Museum of Photography's Web page for K-12 kids has an

Interactive Gallery, Media Literacy Program, and Lesson Plans.

○ **Museums http://www.comlab.ox.ac.uk/archive/other/museums.html** From the WWW Virtual Library. Has links to museums, exhibits, galleries, libraries, and further lists and links.

○ **Le Louvre, http://mistral.enst.fr/~pioch/louvre/** You guessed it. Oui, Oui, Parlez-vous francais?

SCIENCE AND MATH

○ **Kid's Science Newsletter http://www.ceismc.gatech.edu/kidsclub/title.htm** Thanks to Peggie Scott for telling us about this great site—a great science newsletter for kid's!

○ **Nye Labs Online http://nyelabs.kcts.org** Bill Nye the Science Guy.

○ **Helping Your Kids Learn Science http://www.ed.gov/pubs/parents/Science/index.html** For parents. Do your kids ask: Why is the sky blue? Why do things fall to the ground? How do seeds grow? What makes sound and music? Where do mountains come from? Well, look into this from the government.

○ **VolcanoWorld http://volcano.und.nodak.edu/** Everything about volcanoes. Includes a Hawaiian Tour Guide, volcano images, current and recent eruptions, and more.

○ **The Snow Page http://rmd-www.mr.ic.ac.uk/snow/snowpage.html** Covers every aspect of the white fluffy stuff. Everything from snowboarding to travels, magazines, trails, you name it.

○ **NASA/JPL Imaging Radar Home Page http://southport.jpl.nasa.gov** Images, video and animation to bring the next Space Shuttle mission to living room.

Pen Pals

○ **Canadian International Penfriends http://www.magic. mb.ca/~lampi/snailmail/ipl.html**

Terms You Will Need

Introduction to Smileys, Emoticons, and Acronyms

Sometimes it's hard to say what you mean by just using words. We often use facial expressions and hand gestures to punctuate our words, especially in a serious discussion. When using the computer to communicate, body language and voice inflection—the verbal and nonverbal clues that normally go with a face-to-face or telephone conversation—are lacking. Without those expressions, online messages can seem a bit impersonal to some users. This can easily lead to misunderstandings, hurt feelings, or even a complete loss of meaning. A comment made in jest can be taken literally and lead to disastrous results.

Users, however, can personalize their messages by adding some written clues. One way users can convey emotion is by adding stage directions. For example, <grin> or <sad> typed at the end of a paragraph will emphasize how you feel. Any emotion can be added to the end of a statement in this way to help people understand what you mean. Many common emotions are shortened up to a single letter. For instance <g> stands for grin or <s> stands for sad.

Another method for adding emotion to a message is by using Smileys or emoticons. These are formed by keystrokes from the keyboard that to the uninitiated are meaningless garbage—but turn this page 90° clockwise and look at each of these symbols.

Common Smileys

The following are from "The Unofficial Smiley Dictionary" available on America Online as Emoticons.txt:

:-)	Smile with a nose
:)	Smile without a nose
;-)	You are winking
:-(	You are unhappy
:-I	You are indifferent
:->	Biting sarcastic remark
>:->	Devilish remark
:-°	You ate something sour
:'-(	You are crying
:-@	You are screaming
:<)	You are from an Ivy League School
:-&	You are tongue tied
-:-)	You are a punk rocker
-:-(	(real punk rockers don't smile)
O :-)	You are an angel (at heart, at least)

:-P	Sticking tongue out
:-D	Laughing (at you!)
:-o	Uh oh!
<:-I	You are a dunce
—-<—{(@	Its a Rose!

See, this can be fun. There are hundreds of these smileys. Go ahead, make one up yourself. You never know what might catch on.

One final set of definitions that make discussions online much easier are acronyms. These are just shortcuts that are used extensively in chat groups, newsgroups, and email.

Some common acronyms are:

AAMOF	As a Matter of Fact
BBFN	Bye Bye for Now
BTW	By the Way
BYKT	But You Knew That
CMIIW	Correct Me if I'm Wrong
EOL	End of Lecture
FITB	Fill in the Blank
IAC	In Any Case
ILY	I Love You
IMHO	In My Humble Opinion
IRL	In Real Life
LJBF	Let's Just be Friends
LOL	Laugh Out Loud

OIC	Oh! I See
OTOH	On the Other Hand
TIC	Tongue in Cheek
TTFN	Ta Ta for Now
TYVM	Thank You Very Much

Regardless of whether you use smileys, stage directions or acronyms, the important thing to remember when communicating online is to be yourself, use common sense, and mind your manners.

Common Definitions

ASCII
An acronym that stands for American Standard Code for Information Interchange. This standard represents text, punctuation and other characters numerically so that ASCII files can be read by any computers word processor.

Acronyms
Shortcuts in which a phrase is represented by its initials. (i.e. WWW - World Wide Web)

Address
A unique string of characters that defines your location in cyberspace—just like your home address is unique to you. Note that addresses are case specific so don't get your caps and lowercase mixed up.

Alias
Sometimes a computer command, an Internet site name, or another computer name can be very long or complicated. To simplify execution of the command or access the name, some programs let you create an alias. When you type the alias, the full command or name is executed or referenced.

Archie	A network service used to locate files publicly accessible by anonymous File Transfer Protocol (FTP). There are approximately 30 Archie servers in the world.
BBS	*(Bulletin Board System)* One or more computers made available to other users via phone lines. Depending on how many modems are in the BBS's computer(s), multiple users can access information on the BBS' computer. Conceptually, the Internet can be viewed as a huge BBS.
bps	*(bits per second)* Refers to the speed at which a particular modem can transmit data.
Bandwidth	The range of transmission frequencies that a network can use. The greater the bandwidth, the greater the amount of information that can travel on the network at a time
Baud	*(Baud rate)* The measure of speed that data can be transmitted down a channel (a telephone line or serial cable), roughly equivalent to bits per second. Modems are often rated by baud rates. For example, a 14,400 baud modem can send data at approximately 14,400 bits per second.
Binary	An on/off numerical system used by computers where 1's are on and 0's are off. Using binary code, every combination of letters and symbols are represented in your computers memory.
Bookmarks	To facilitate easier access to known sites with lengthy addresses, most browsers and other access programs allow you to create a *marker* or *pointer* to a particular address, called a bookmark. Once the

bookmark is created, simply click on the bookmark to access the associated Internet address.

Boolean Logic   A system for searching and retrieving information from computers by using and combining terms such as AND, OR, and NOT to sort data.

Cable   A bundle of wires with connectors on the ends, such as phone cables, serial cables, and disk drive cables.

Chat Room   Areas where users meet to have real-time interactive conversations via the keyboard similar to telephone conference calls.

Click   When you point at something on your screen with your mouse and press down with your mouse button.

Client   A computer with access to network services. Computers that provide services are "servers." A user at a client may request file access, remote log-in, file transfer, printing or other available services from servers.

Commercial Service Provider   Services such as American Online, CompuServe, Delphi, and Prodigy that have gateways into the Internet. Any of these services are a good way to start surfing the Net, since their simple icons make it easy to get help online. They also offer access to their other services as well, including email, for which they provide the software.

Communications Parameters   A setting or series of settings required to enable a computer to communicate. Some examples of settings are parity, stop bits, data bits, and duplex.

Communications Port
A socket on the back of the computer for hooking up devices such as mice or modems.

Compression
The reduction of computer data size so less data is needed to represent the same information and therefore take up less disk or file space and may be transmitted in less time.

Configuration
(1) A general-purpose term that refers to how your computer is set up. (2) The total combination of hardware components—central processing unit, video display device, keyboard, and peripheral devices—that make up a computer system. (3) The software settings that allow various hardware components of a computer system to communicate with one another.

Configure
To change software or hardware actions by changing settings. Configurations can be set or reset in software or by manipulating hardware jumpers, switches, or other elements.

Connect Time
The amount of time a user is connected to an online information service.

Cursor
A blinking line on your screen that indicates where the next character you type will be inserted.

Cyberspace
The virtual universe created when people interact via computers. Being on the Internet is also known as being in Cyberspace. While each user accessing the Internet is in a physical location, all the users hooked together by their computers comprise Cyberspace.

Data
Information that is processed or stored by a computer program, including text, numbers, program code, graphic art, sound, or even video clips.

Databases	Large collections of data. A school system might maintain a database of information relating to the students, faculty, physical buildings, etc.
Data Bits	A communications parameter that indicates the size of each character. Computers use a character to represent a letter, numeral, or symbol in the digital 0s and 1s they can understand. Characters are usually seven or eight bits long.
Data Encryption	The scheme by which information is transformed into random streams of bits to create a secret code for data security.
Directory	A subdivided list of data stored on hard drives and floppy disks. Comparing a directory to a file cabinet, the directories on a disk are like the drawers. The files in the directory are like the file folders inside the drawer.
Download	Receiving information from another computer. (See **upload**)
Domain Name	A name given to one of the networks that make up the Internet is called a domain. On a single domain are a number of individual addresses called Domain names.
Duplex	A communications parameter that determines how the keystrokes you type appear on-screen. *Half duplex* means that your keystrokes appear as a direct result of your typing them. *Full duplex* means that keystrokes appear as a result of the modem to which you are connected echoing them back to you as a method of confirmation.
Electronic Mail (email)	Message sent electronically from one computer to another.

It can be sent from one office to another in a local area network (LAN) or from one side of the world to the other on the Internet or via other online service providers.

Emoticons
Emotion icons. When you type a message on the Internet, the reader may not understand the emotion you're trying to convey. For example, you may type something as a joke, but the reader takes it seriously. Placing emoticons in the text shows that you are just kidding. For example, <g> means grin, ; >) is a smile, ; > (is a frown.

FAQ
Frequently Asked Questions Pronounced "fack." A list of the most common questions likely to be asked about a certain subject and their answers. These file's names usually end with .faq and are used extensively on the Internet.

FTP
(File Transfer Protocol) A protocol which determines how files are transferred from one computer to another.

File
Any named, ordered collection of information stored on a disk. For example, application programs and operating systems on disks. You make a file when you create text or graphics, give the material a name, and save it to disk; in this sense, file is synonymous with document. (See **directory**)

File Server
A computer on which users can store files and applications. The Internet is a network of file servers.

Flame
Writing or posting unkind remarks in response to something someone has posted online or sent through email.

Forum	On CompuServe, America Online or Prodigy, a specific place for discussing a certain subject. (See **Newsgroups**)
Freeware	Software that has been placed into the public domain and can be downloaded and used for free.
Front End	A non-technical term that describes the user interface to a computer application or solution. It implies a "back-end" that the user never sees that actually performs the desired function.
Gateway	A connection between two incompatible applications or networks so that data can be transferred.
Gateway server	Computers that allow access to the Internet.
GIF	(*Graphic Interchange Format*) Pronounced "jiff." A commonly used format developed by CompuServe to store photo-quality graphic images.
Gopher	A menu-based means of exploring information resources.
Gopher server	A computer on the Internet that is set up to service information requests issued by the Gopher program to help you find information on the Internet.
Hacker	One who works to gain unauthorized access to software or computer systems through trial and error.
Handshake	What two modems do first when trying to connect so that they can transfer data the same way.
Home Page	A home page is the initial document shown when a user accesses a web site.

Host Computer   (1) A multiuser computer, such as a minicomputer or mainframe, that serves as a central processing unit for a number of terminals. (2) A computer that receives information from and sends data to terminals over telecommunication lines. The computer in control in a data communication network.

Hyperlink   The connection address used in hypertext documents to jump from one element to another.

Hypertext   Specially formatted text used primarily in World Wide Web documents thatis used to create links between documentsa. Choosing this text will jump you to the linked information source.

HyperText Markup Language   *(HTML)* The programming language used to create hyperlinks on the Web.

Icon   A small image on the computer screen that executes a program or a function within a larger program when you point and click on it. Each icon represents a particular program or function in the software.

Internet   (1) A network of two of more interconnected local area or wide area networks. (2) A world-wide interconnected group of networks.

Internet address   An address for a computer on a network consisting of a network number and a host number that is unique for that network.

Internet Service Provider   An organization that provides connections to the Internet.

Knowbot   *(Knowledge robot)* A software program that retrieves information.

Links
Addresses inserted into hypertext documents that let you jump to another document.

Local Area Network (LAN)
A group of computers connected for the purpose of sharing resources, typically joined by a single transmission cable, and located within a small area, such as a single building or section of a building.

Login Name
The name required to enter a computer network.

Log Off
To indicate to a system or network that you have completed your work and are terminating interaction.

Log On
To indicate to a system or network that you are starting your work and beginning interaction. Often requires a password.

Lurking
Being connected to an online service but watching without getting involved. Most people lurk when they first enter a new area on the Internet. Delurking is the opposite of lurking.

Modem
(**MO**dulater/**DEM**odulator) A device that lets a PC communicate and exchange information with other modem-equipped computers via telephone lines.

Net
Short for Internet.

Netiquette
The etiquette to be followed when accessing the Internet. An unwritten set of rules governing how one should act when accessing the Internet.

Network
A collection of interconnected, individually controlled computers and the hardware and software used to connect them. A network allows users to share data and peripheral devices (such as

	printers and storage media) and exchange electronic mail.
Newbie	A name given to new Internet users.
Newsgroups	A forum for groups of people with common interests who meet online for discussion. There are newsgroups for every issue imaginable online. Messages are posted for all to read and respond to.
Newsreader	A software program that is usually part of your Internet service package. It lets you read the news available in newsgroups.
Offline	Not currently connected to a network.
Online	Currently connected to a network.
Parity	A communications parameter used to perform an error-checking procedure. Modems must agree on the parity they will use prior to the start of communications. With even parity, the character must have an even number of digital 1s to be deemed error free by the receiving modem. With odd parity the character must have an odd number of 1s.
Peripheral	A device attached to a computer or network, such as a printer or modem, that aren't necessary for the computer to run but serve a much need purpose.
Public Domain	Referes to that which is without defined ownership or copyright. Information that is usually free to anyone who wants to download it.
RJ–11 Cable	A standard telephone wire with small plastic jacks that fits into RJ–11 ports typically located in the wall or floor, on the back of a telephone, and the back of a modem.

Readme File   Often found on FTP sites or with computer software,
they explain the contents of an FTP directory or
additional facts not in the printed instruction manuals.

Remote Computer A computer connected to another computer or
network via telephone lines (or other network
connection).

Search Engines   A program designed to search the Internet for user
requested information.

Search Words   Words you enter in a search engine to help you find
a document. Documents are often coded with key
search words that are then matched up by a search
engine, and the document is returned.

Server   A computer that provides a particular service across
a network, including file access, login access, file
transfer, printing.

Shareware   Software distributed on a free trial basis. If you like
it, you send a licensing fee to the author of the
program. The honor system applies, as there
generally is no way for the author to determine who
is using his or her program.

Signature   A text file, usually five lines or less, containing your
identification and any contact information added to
your network news articles and email messages.

Site   The physical location of a computer, sometimes
referring to where a computer is located on the
Internet. For instance, when you go to Safety Net's
site, you are going to the place where it stores its
documents and maintains its home page.

Snail mail   A less-than-favorable reference to the mail
delivered by the U.S. Postal Service.

SPAM

(Sending Particularly Annoying Messages) Sending an article everywhere on the Internet, rather than just to specific groups that it might interest.

Stop Bit

A communications parameter that marks the end of a character. There's usually only one stop bit, though sometimes there can be two.

Surfing

Jumping around from site to site on the Internet.

Sysop

(**SYS**tem **Op**erator) Someone who runs a computer system or bulletin board.

TELNET

A terminal emulation protocol that lets you login remotely to other computers on the Internet.

Terminal

A keyboard and display screen through which users can access a host computer.

Threads

Discussions about a common subject within a Newsgroup or mailing list. To follow a thread means to start with the first message and work your way through subsequent messages in response.

URL

(Uniform Resource Locator) An address for the location of any Internet resource, whether it is a single file on an FTP site, an entire Gopher server, or an image on the Web.

USENET

A network of about three million users that communicate through a collection of newsgroups devoted to particular interests. There is a Usenet Newsgroup for almost any imaginable topic.

Veronica

A search tool accessible through a Gopher program which allows you to quickly scan Gopher sites for particular files and directories.

213

Web Browsers   Programs that let you navigate through the World Wide Web and see graphics and text on your computer screen. They also allow you to make hypertext leaps to other Web sites.

Wide Area   *(WAN)* Computers and/or networks connected via long

Network   distance communication methods, such as telephone lines and satellites.

World Wide Web   *(WWW)* A hypertext-based Internet systemfor browsing Internet resources.

Government Censorship or Parental Monitoring

In January of 1996, the United States Congress passed a bill entitled the Telecommunications Reform Act of 1996. This act has had sweeping effects on the communications industry, which will also greatly impact the general public.

What many people did not know was that buried deep within the language of this bill was a stipulation called the Communications Decency Act that would make it illegal to knowingly transmit to a minor indecent or patently offensive material. On the face of things, this may not seem like a bad approach to an acknowledged affront to children in this country and others.

However, the bill caused several major problems that ultimately resulted in the filing of a class action suit by the American Civil Liberties Union and other plaintiffs who charged that the bill violated First Amendment rights to free speech.

215

Prior to hearing the case, a panel of three federal judges agreed that a thorough understanding of the Internet's functionality would be required in order to hear the case. For several months, experts from around the world testified as to what the Internet is and how it functions.

What follows is the **Findings of Fact**, an excerpt from the judges' ruling that summarizes the months of testimony regarding what the Internet is, the content that is available on the Internet, the issues regarding inappropriate material on the Internet and the options available to control such material.

Hopefully, you will find it useful as an additional reference about the Internet and a reminder of why mom and dad make much better monitors than Big Brother.

II. Finding of Fact

All parties agree that in order to apprehend the legal questions at issue in these cases, it is necessary to have a clear understanding of the exponentially growing, worldwide medium that is the Internet, which presents unique issues relating to the application of First Amendment jurisprudence and due process requirements to this new and evolving method of communication. For this reason all parties insisted on having extensive evidentiary hearings before the three-judge court. The court's Findings of fact are made pursuant to Fed. R. Civ. P. 52(a). The history and basic technology of this medium are not in dispute, and the first forty-eight paragraphs of the following Findings of fact are derived from the like-numbered paragraphs of a stipulation(8) the parties filed with the court.(9)

The Nature of Cyberspace

THE CREATION OF THE INTERNET AND THE DEVELOPMENT OF CYBERSPACE

1. The Internet is not a physical or tangible entity, but rather a giant network which interconnects innumerable smaller groups of

linked computer networks. It is thus a network of networks. This is best understood if one considers what a linked group of computers—referred to here as a "network"—is, and what it does. Small networks are now ubiquitous (and are often called "local area networks"). For example, in many United States courthouses, computers are linked to each other for the purpose of exchanging files and messages (and to share equipment such as printers). These are networks.

2. Some networks are "closed" networks, not linked to other computers or networks. Many networks, however, are connected to other networks, which are in turn connected to other networks in a manner which permits each computer in any network to communicate with computers on any other network in the system. This global Web of linked networks and computers is referred to as the Internet.

3. The nature of the Internet is such that it is very difficult, if not impossible, to determine its size at a given moment. It is indisputable, however, that the Internet has experienced extraordinary growth in recent years. In 1981, fewer than 300 computers were linked to the Internet, and by 1989, the number stood at fewer than 90,000 computers. By 1993, over 1,000,000 computers were linked. Today, over 9,400,000 host computers worldwide, of which approximately 60 percent located within the United States are estimated to be linked to the Internet. This count does not include the personal computers people use to access the Internet using modems. In all, reasonable estimates are that as many as 40 million people around the world can and do access the enormously flexible communication Internet medium. That figure is expected to grow to 200 million Internet users by the year 1999.

4. Some of the computers and computer networks that make up the Internet are owned by governmental and public institutions, some are owned by non-profit organizations, and some are privately owned. The resulting whole is a decentralized, global medium of communications or "cyberspace" that links people, institutions, corporations,

and governments around the world. The Internet is an international system. This communications medium allows any of the literally tens of millions of people with access to the Internet to exchange information. These communications can occur almost instantaneously, and can be directed either to specific individuals, to a broader group of people interested in a particular subject, or to the world as a whole.

5. The Internet had its origins in 1969 as an experimental project of the Advanced Research Project Agency ("ARPA"), and was called ARPANET. This network linked computers and computer networks owned by the military, defense contractors, and university laboratories conducting defense-related research. The network later allowed researchers across the country to access directly and to use extremely powerful supercomputers located at a few key universities and laboratories. As it evolved far beyond its research origins in the United States to encompass universities, corporations, and people around the world, the ARPANET came to be called the "DARPA Internet," and finally just the "Internet."

6. From its inception, the network was designed to be a decentralized, self-maintaining series of redundant links between computers and computer networks, capable of rapidly transmitting communications without direct human involvement or control, and with the automatic ability to re-route communications if one or more individual links were damaged or otherwise unavailable. Among other goals, this redundant system of linked computers was designed to allow vital research and communications to continue even if portions of the network were damaged, say, in a war.

7. To achieve this resilient nationwide (and ultimately global) communications medium, the ARPANET encouraged the creation of multiple links to and from each computer (or computer network) on the network. Thus, a computer located in Washington, D.C., might be linked (usually using dedicated telephone lines) to other computers in neighboring states or on the Eastern seaboard. Each of those computers could in turn be linked to other computers, which themselves would be linked to other computers.

8.   A communication sent over this redundant series of linked computers could travel any of a number of routes to its destination. Thus, a message sent from a computer in Washington, D.C., to a computer in Palo Alto, California, might first be sent to a computer in Philadelphia, and then be forwarded to a computer in Pittsburgh, and then to Chicago, Denver, and Salt Lake City, before finally reaching Palo Alto. If the message could not travel along that path (because of military attack, simple technical malfunction, or other reason), the message would automatically (without human intervention or even knowledge) be re-routed, perhaps, from Washington, D.C. to Richmond, and then to Atlanta, New Orleans, Dallas, Albuquerque, Los Angeles, and finally to Palo Alto. This type of transmission, and re-routing, would likely occur in a matter of seconds.

9.   Messages between computers on the Internet do not necessarily travel entirely along the same path. The Internet uses "packet switching" communication protocols that allow individual messages to be subdivided into smaller "packets" that are then sent independently to the destination, and are then automatically reassembled by the receiving computer. While all packets of a given message often travel along the same path to the destination, if computers along the route become overloaded, then packets can be re-routed to less loaded computers.

10. At the same time that ARPANET was maturing (it subsequently ceased to exist), similar networks developed to link universities, research facilities, businesses, and individuals around the world. These other formal or loose networks included BITNET, CSNET, FIDONET, and USENET. Eventually, each of these networks (many of which overlapped) were themselves linked together, allowing users of any computers linked to any one of the networks to transmit communications to users of computers on other networks. It is this series of linked networks (themselves linking computers and computer networks) that is today commonly known as the Internet.

11. No single entity—academic, corporate, governmental, or non-profit—administers the Internet. It exists and functions as a result of the fact that hundreds of thousands of separate operators of computers and computer networks independently decided to use common data transfer protocols to exchange communications and information with other computers (which in turn exchange communications and information with still other computers). There is no centralized storage location, control point, or communications channel for the Internet, and it would not be technically feasible for a single entity to control all of the information conveyed on the Internet.

How Individuals Access the Internet

12. Individuals have a wide variety of avenues to access cyberspace in general, and the Internet in particular. In terms of physical access, there are two common methods to establish an actual link to the Internet. First, one can use a computer or computer terminal that is directly (and usually permanently) connected to a computer network that is itself directly or indirectly connected to the Internet. Second, one can use a "personal computer" with a "modem" to connect over a telephone line to a larger computer or computer network that is itself directly or indirectly connected to the Internet. As detailed below, both direct and modem connections are made available to people by a wide variety of academic, governmental, or commercial entities.

13. Students, faculty, researchers, and others affiliated with the vast majority of colleges and universities in the United States can access the Internet through their educational institutions. Such access is often via direct connection using computers located in campus libraries, offices, or computer centers, or may be through telephone access using a modem from a student's or professor's campus or off-campus location. Some colleges and universities

install "ports" or outlets for direct network connections in each dormitory room or provide access via computers located in common areas in dormitories. Such access enables students and professors to use information and content provided by the college or university itself, and to use the vast amount of research resources and other information available on the Internet worldwide.

14. Similarly, Internet resources and access are sufficiently important to many corporations and other employers that those employers link their office computer networks to the Internet and provide employees with direct or modem access to the office network (and thus to the Internet). Such access might be used by, for example, a corporation involved in scientific or medical research or manufacturing to enable corporate employees to exchange information and ideas with academic researchers in their fields.

15. Those who lack access to the Internet through their schools or employers still have a variety of ways they can access the Internet. Many communities across the country have established "free-nets" or community networks to provide their citizens with a local link to the Internet (and to provide local-oriented content and discussion groups). The first such community network, the Cleveland Free-Net Community Computer System, was established in 1986, and free-nets now exist in scores of communities as diverse as Richmond, Virginia, Tallahassee, Florida, Seattle, Washington, and San Diego, California. Individuals typically can access free-nets at little or no cost via modem connection or by using computers available in community buildings. Free-nets are often operated by a local library, educational institution, or nonprofit community group.

16. Individuals can also access the Internet through many local libraries. Libraries often offer patrons use of computers that are linked to the Internet. In addition, some libraries offer telephone modem access to the libraries' computers, which are themselves connected to the Internet. Increasingly, patrons now use library

services and resources without ever physically entering the library itself. Libraries typically provide such direct or modem access at no cost to the individual user.

17. Individuals can also access the Internet by patronizing an increasing number of storefront "computer coffee shops," where customers—while they drink their coffee—can use computers provided by the shop to access the Internet. Such Internet access is typically provided by the shop for a small hourly fee.

18. Individuals can also access the Internet through commercial and non-commercial "Internet service providers" that typically offer modem telephone access to a computer or computer network linked to the Internet. Many such providers—including the members of plaintiff Commercial Internet Exchange Association—are commercial entities offering Internet access for a monthly or hourly fee. Some Internet service providers, however, are non-profit organizations that offer free or very low cost access to the Internet. For example, the International Internet Association offers free modem access to the Internet upon request. Also, a number of trade or other non-profit associations offer Internet access as a service to members.

19. Another common way for individuals to access the Internet is through one of the major national commercial "online services" such as America Online, CompuServe, the Microsoft Network, or Prodigy. These online services offer nationwide computer networks (so that subscribers can dial-in to a local telephone number), and the services provide extensive and well organized content within their own proprietary computer networks. In addition to allowing access to the extensive content available within each online service, the services also allow subscribers to link to the much larger resources of the Internet. Full access to the online service (including access to the Internet) can be obtained for modest monthly or hourly fees. The major commercial online services have almost twelve million individual subscribers across the United States.

20. In addition to using the national commercial online services, individuals can also access the Internet using some (but not all) of the thousands of local dial-in computer services, often called "bulletin board systems" or "BBSs." With an investment of as little as $2,000.00 and the cost of a telephone line, individuals, non-profit organizations, advocacy groups, and businesses can offer their own dial-in computer "bulletin board" service where friends, members, subscribers, or customers can exchange ideas and information. BBSs range from single computers with only one telephone line into the computer (allowing only one user at a time), to single computers with many telephone lines into the computer (allowing multiple simultaneous users), to multiple linked computers each servicing multiple dial-in telephone lines (allowing multiple simultaneous users). Some (but not all) of these BBS systems offer direct or indirect links to the Internet. Some BBS systems charge users a nominal fee for access, while many others are free to the individual users.

21. Although commercial access to the Internet is growing rapidly, many users of the Internet—such as college students and staff—do not individually pay for access (except to the extent, for example, that the cost of computer services is a component of college tuition). These and other Internet users can access the Internet without paying for such access with a credit card or other form of payment.

Methods to Communicate Over the Internet

22. Once one has access to the Internet, there are a wide variety of different methods of communication and information exchange over the network. These many methods of communication and information retrieval are constantly evolving and are therefore difficult to categorize concisely. The most common methods of communications on the Internet (as well as within the major

online services) can be roughly grouped into six categories:

(1) one-to-one messaging (such as "e-mail"),

(2) one-to-many messaging (such as "listserv"),

(3) distributed message databases (such as "USENET news-groups"),

(4) real time communication (such as "Internet Relay Chat"),

(5) real time remote computer utilization (such as "telnet"), and

(6) remote information retrieval (such as "ftp," "gopher," and the "World Wide Web").

Most of these methods of communication can be used to transmit text, data, computer programs, sound, visual images (i.e., pictures), and moving video images.

23. One-to-one messaging. One method of communication on the Internet is via electronic mail, or "e-mail," comparable in principle to sending a first class letter. One can address and transmit a message to one or more other people. E-mail on the Internet is not routed through a central control point, and can take many and varying paths to the recipients. Unlike postal mail, simple e-mail generally is not "sealed" or secure, and can be accessed or viewed on intermediate computers between the sender and recipient (unless the message is encrypted).

24. One-to-many messaging. The Internet also contains automatic mailing list services (such as "listservs"), [also referred to by witnesses as "mail exploders"] that allow communications about particular subjects of interest to a group of people. For example, people can subscribe to a "listserv" mailing list on a particular topic of interest to them. The subscriber can submit messages on the topic to the listserv that are forwarded (via e-mail), either automatically or through a human moderator overseeing the listserv, to anyone who has subscribed to the mailing list. A recipient of such a message can reply to the message and have the reply

also distributed to everyone on the mailing list. This service provides the capability to keep abreast of developments or events in a particular subject area. Most listserv-type mailing lists automatically forward all incoming messages to all mailing list subscribers. There are thousands of such mailing list services on the Internet, collectively with hundreds of thousands of subscribers. Users of "open" listservs typically can add or remove their names from the mailing list automatically, with no direct human involvement. Listservs may also be "closed," i.e., only allowing for one's acceptance into the listserv by a human moderator.

25. Distributed message databases. Similar in function to listservs— but quite different in how communications are transmitted—are distributed message databases such as "USENET newsgroups." User-sponsored newsgroups are among the most popular and widespread applications of Internet services, and cover all imaginable topics of interest to users. Like listservs, newsgroups are open discussions and exchanges on particular topics. Users, however, need not subscribe to the discussion mailing list in advance, but can instead access the database at any time. Some USENET newsgroups are "moderated" but most are open access. For the moderated newsgroups,(10) all messages to the newsgroup are forwarded to one person who can screen them for relevance to the topics under discussion. USENET newsgroups are disseminated using ad hoc, peer to peer connections between approximately 200,000 computers (called USENET "servers") around the world. For unmoderated newsgroups, when an individual user with access to a USENET server posts a message to a newsgroup, the message is automatically forwarded to all adjacent USENET servers that furnish access to the newsgroup, and it is then propagated to the servers adjacent to those servers, etc. The messages are temporarily stored on each receiving server, where they are available for review and response by individual users. The messages are automatically and periodically purged from each system after a time to make room for new messages.

Responses to messages, like the original messages, are automatically distributed to all other computers receiving the newsgroup or forwarded to a moderator in the case of a moderated newsgroup. The dissemination of messages to USENET servers around the world is an automated process that does not require direct human intervention or review.

26. There are newsgroups on more than fifteen thousand different subjects. In 1994, approximately 70,000 messages were posted to newsgroups each day, and those messages were distributed to the approximately 190,000 computers or computer networks that participate in the USENET newsgroup system. Once the messages reach the approximately 190,000 receiving computers or computer networks, they are available to individual users of those computers or computer networks. Collectively, almost 100,000 new messages (or "articles") are posted to newsgroups each day.

27. Real time communication. In addition to transmitting messages that can be later read or accessed, individuals on the Internet can engage in an immediate dialog, in "real time", with other people on the Internet. In its simplest forms, "talk" allows one-to-one communications and "Internet Relay Chat" (or IRC) allows two or more to type messages to each other that almost immediately appear on the others' computer screens. IRC is analogous to a telephone party line, using a computer and keyboard rather than a telephone. With IRC, however, at any one time there are thousands of different party lines available, in which collectively tens of thousands of users are engaging in conversations on a huge range of subjects. Moreover, one can create a new party line to discuss a different topic at any time. Some IRC conversations are "moderated" or include "channel operators."

28. In addition, commercial online services such as America Online, CompuServe, the Microsoft Network, and Prodigy have their own "chat" systems allowing their members to converse.

29. Real time remote computer utilization. Another method to use information on the Internet is to access and control remote computers in "real time" using "telnet." For example, using telnet, a researcher at a university would be able to use the computing power of a supercomputer located at a different university. A student can use telnet to connect to a remote library to access the library's online card catalog program.

30. Remote information retrieval. The final major category of communication may be the most well known use of the Internet—the search for and retrieval of information located on remote computers. There are three primary methods to locate and retrieve information on the Internet.

31. A simple method uses "ftp" (or file transfer protocol) to list the names of computer files available on a remote computer, and to transfer one or more of those files to an individual's local computer.

32. Another approach uses a program and format named "gopher" to guide an individual's search through the resources available on a remote computer.

The World Wide Web

33. A third approach, and fast becoming the most well-known on the Internet, is the "World Wide Web." The Web utilizes a "hypertext" formatting language called hypertext markup language (HTML), and programs that "browse" the Web can display HTML documents containing text, images, sound, animation and moving video. Any HTML document can include links to other types of information or resources, so that while viewing an HTML document that, for example, describes resources available on the Internet, one can "click" using a computer mouse on the description of the resource and be immediately connected to the

resource itself. Such "hyperlinks" allow information to be accessed and organized in very flexible ways, and allow people to locate and efficiently view related information even if the information is stored on numerous computers all around the world.

34. Purpose. The World Wide Web (W3C) was created to serve as the platform for a global, online store of knowledge, containing information from a diversity of sources and accessible to Internet users around the world. Though information on the Web is contained in individual computers, the fact that each of these computers is connected to the Internet through W3C protocols allows all of the information to become part of a single body of knowledge. It is currently the most advanced information system developed on the Internet, and embraces within its data model most information in previous networked information systems such as ftp, gopher, wais, and Usenet.

35. History. W3C was originally developed at CERN, the European Particle Physics Laboratory, and was initially used to allow information sharing within internationally dispersed teams of researchers and engineers. Originally aimed at the High Energy Physics community, it has spread to other areas and attracted much interest in user support, resource recovery, and many other areas which depend on collaborative and information sharing. The Web has extended beyond the scientific and academic community to include communications by individuals, non-profit organizations, and businesses.

36. Basic Operation. The World Wide Web is a series of documents stored in different computers all over the Internet. Documents contain information stored in a variety of formats, including text, still images, sounds, and video. An essential element of the Web is that any document has an address (rather like a telephone number). Most Web documents contain "links." These are short sections of text or image which refer to another document. Typically the linked text is blue or underlined when displayed,

and when selected by the user, the referenced document is automatically displayed, wherever in the world it actually is stored. Links for example are used to lead from overview documents to more detailed documents, from tables of contents to particular pages, but also as cross-references, footnotes, and new forms of information structure.

37. Many organizations now have "home pages" on the Web. These are documents which provide a set of links designed to represent the organization, and through links from the home page, guide the user directly or indirectly to information about or relevant to that organization.

38. As an example of the use of links, if these Findings were to be put on a World Wide Web site, its home page might contain links such as those:

○ THE NATURE OF CYBERSPACE

○ CREATION OF THE INTERNET AND THE DEVELOP-MENT OF CYBERSPACE

○ HOW PEOPLE ACCESS THE INTERNET

○ METHODS TO COMMUNICATE OVER THE INTERNET

39. Each of these links takes the user of the site from the beginning of the Findings to the appropriate section within this Adjudication. Links may also take the user from the original Web site to another Web site on another computer connected to the Internet. These links from one computer to another, from one document to another across the Internet, are what unify the Web into a single body of knowledge, and what makes the Web unique. The Web was designed with a maximum target time to follow a link of one tenth of a second.

40. Publishing. The World Wide Web exists fundamentally as a platform through which people and organizations can communicate

through shared information. When information is made available, it is said to be "published" on the Web. Publishing on the Web simply requires that the "publisher" has a computer connected to the Internet and that the computer is running W3C server software. The computer can be as simple as a small personal computer costing less than $1500 dollars or as complex as a multi-million dollar mainframe computer. Many Web publishers choose instead to lease disk storage space from someone else who has the necessary computer facilities, eliminating the need for actually owning any equipment oneself.

41. The Web, as a universe of network accessible information, contains a variety of documents prepared with quite varying degrees of care, from the hastily typed idea, to the professionally executed corporate profile. The power of the Web stems from the ability of a link to point to any document, regardless of its status or physical location.

42. Information to be published on the Web must also be formatted according to the rules of the Web standards. These standardized formats assure that all Web users who want to read the material will be able to view it. Web standards are sophisticated and flexible enough that they have grown to meet the publishing needs of many large corporations, banks, brokerage houses, newspapers and magazines which now publish "online" editions of their material, as well as government agencies, and even courts, which use the Web to disseminate information to the public. At the same time, Web publishing is simple enough that thousands of individual users and small community organizations are using the Web to publish their own personal "home pages," the equivalent of individualized newsletters about that person or organization, which are available to everyone on the Web.

43. Web publishers have a choice to make their Web sites open to the general pool of all Internet users, or close them, thus making the information accessible only to those with advance authorization. Many publishers choose to keep their sites open to all in

order to give their information the widest potential audience. In the event that the publishers choose to maintain restrictions on access, this may be accomplished by assigning specific user names and passwords as a prerequisite to access to the site. Or, in the case of Web sites maintained for internal use of one organization, access will only be allowed from other computers within that organization's local network.(11)

44. Searching the Web. A variety of systems have developed that allow users of the Web to search particular information among all of the public sites that are part of the Web. Services such as Yahoo, Magellan, Altavista, Webcrawler, and Lycos are all services known as "search engines" which allow users to search for Web sites that contain certain categories of information, or to search for key words. For example, a Web user looking for the text of Supreme Court opinions would type the words "Supreme Court" into a search engine, and then be presented with a list of World Wide Web sites that contain Supreme Court information. This list would actually be a series of links to those sites. Having searched out a number of sites that might contain the desired information, the user would then follow individual links, browsing through the information on each site, until the desired material is found. For many content providers on the Web, the ability to be found by these search engines is very important.

45. Common standards. The Web links together disparate information on an ever-growing number of Internet-linked computers by setting common information storage formats (HTML) and a common language for the exchange of Web documents (HTTP). Although the information itself may be in many different formats, and stored on computers which are not otherwise compatible, the basic Web standards provide a basic set of standards which allow communication and exchange of information. Despite the fact that many types of computers are used on the Web, and the fact that many of these machines are otherwise incompatible, those

who "publish" information on the Web are able to communicate with those who seek to access information with little difficulty because of these basic technical standards.

46. A distributed system with no centralized control. Running on tens of thousands of individual computers on the Internet, the Web is what is knownas a distributed system. The Web was designed so that organizations with computers containing information can become part of the Web simply by attaching their computers to the Internet and running appropriate World Wide Web software. No single organization controls any membership in the Web, nor is there any single centralized point from which individual Web sites or services can be blocked from the Web. From a user's perspective, it may appear to be a single, integrated system, but in reality it has no centralized control point.

47. Contrast to closed databases. The Web's open, distributed, decentralized nature stands in sharp contrast to most information systems that have come before it. Private information services such as Westlaw, Lexis/Nexis, and Dialog, have contained large storehouses of knowledge, and can be accessed from the Internet with the appropriate passwords and access software. However, these databases are not linked together into a single whole, as is the World Wide Web.

48. Success of the Web in research, education, and political activities. The World Wide Web has become so popular because of its open, distributed, and easy-to-use nature. Rather than requiring those who seek information to purchase new software or hardware, and to learn a new kind of system for each new database of information they seek to access, the Web environment makes it easy for users to jump from one set of information to another. By the same token, the open nature of the Web makes it easy for publishers to reach their intended audiences without having to know in advance what kind of computer each potential reader has, and what kind of software they will be using.

Restricting Access to Unwanted On-Line Material(12)

PICS

49. With the rapid growth of the Internet, the increasing popularity of the Web, and the existence of material online that some parents may consider inappropriate for their children, various entities have begun to build systems intended to enable parents to control the material which comes into their homes and may be accessible to their children. The World Wide Web Consortium launched the PICS ("Platform for Internet Content Selection") program in order to develop technical standards that would support parents' ability to filter and screen material that their children see on the Web.

50. The Consortium intends that PICS will provide the ability for third parties, as well as individual content providers, to rate content on the Internet in a variety of ways. When fully implemented, PICS-compatible World Wide Web browsers, Usenet News Group readers, and other Internet applications, will provide parents the ability to choose from a variety of rating services, or a combination of services.

51. PICS working group [PICS-WG] participants include many of the major online services providers, commercial internet access providers, hardware and software companies, major internet content providers, and consumer organizations. Among active participants in the PICS effort are:

Adobe Systems, Inc.

Apple Computer

America Online

AT&T

Center for Democracy and Technology

CompuServe

Delphi Internet Services

Digital Equipment Corporation

IBM

First floor

First Virtual Holdings Incorporated

France Telecom

FTP Software

Industrial Technology Research Institute of Taiwan

Information Technology Association of America

Institut National de Recherche en Informatique et en Automatique (INRIA)

Interactive Services Association

MCI

Microsoft

MIT/LCS/World Wide Web Consortium

NCD

NEC

Netscape Communications Corporation

NewView

O'Reilly and Associates

Open Market

Prodigy Services Company

Progressive Networks

Providence Systems/Parental Guidance

Recreational Software AdvisoryCouncil

SafeSurf

SoftQuad, Inc.

Songline Studios

Spyglass

SurfWatch Software

Telequip Corp.

Time Warner Pathfinder

Viacom Nickelodeon(13)

52. Membership in the PICS-WG includes a broad cross-section of companies from the computer, communications, and content industries, as well as trade associations and public interest groups. PICS technical specifications have been agreed to, allowing the Internet community to begin to deploy products and services based on the PICS-standards.

53. Until a majority of sites on the Internet have been rated by a PICS rating service, PICS will initially function as a "positive" ratings system in which only those sites that have been rated will be displayed using PICS compatible software. In other words, PICS will initially function as a site inclusion list rather than a site exclusion list. The default configuration for a PICS compatible Internet application will be to block access to all sites which have not been rated by a PICS rating service, while allowing access to sites which have a PICS rating for appropriate content.(14)

Software

54. For over a year, various companies have marketed stand alone software that is intended to enable parents and other adults to limit the Internet access of children. Examples of such software include: Cyber Patrol, CYBERsitter, The Internet Filter, Net Nanny, Parental Guidance, SurfWatch, Netscape Proxy Server, and WebTrack. The market for this type of software is growing, and there is increasing competition among software providers to provide products.

Cyber Patrol

55. As more people, particularly children, began to use the Internet, Microsystems Software, Inc. decided to develop and market Internet software intended to empower parents to exercise individual choice over what material their children could access. Microsystems' stated intent is to develop a product which would give parents comfort that their children can reap the benefits of the Internet while shielding them from objectionable or otherwise inappropriate materials based on the parents' own particular tastes and values. Microsystems' product, Cyber Patrol, was developed to address this need.

56. Cyber Patrol was first introduced in August 1995, and is currently available in Windows and Macintosh versions. Cyber Patrol works with both direct Internet Access providers (ISPs, e.g., Netcom, PSI, UUnet), and Commercial Online Service Providers (e.g., America Online, Compuserv, Prodigy, Microsoft). Cyber Patrol is also compatible with all major World Wide Web browsers on the market (e.g., Netscape, Navigator, Mosaic, Prodigy's Legacy and Skimmer browsers, America Online, Netcom's NetCruiser, etc.). Cyber Patrol was the first parental empowerment application to be compatible with the PICS standard. In February of 1996, Microsystems put the first PICS ratings server on the Internet.

57. The CyberNOT list contains approximately 7000 sites in twelve categories. The software is designed to enable parents to selectively block access to any or all of the twelve CyberNOT categories simply by checking boxes in the Cyber Patrol Headquarters (the Cyber Patrol program manager). These categories are:

   ◯ Violence/Profanity: Extreme cruelty, physical or emotional acts against any animal or person which are primarily intended to hurt or inflict pain. Obscene words, phrases, and profanity defined as text that uses George Carlin's seven censored words more often than once every fifty messages or pages.

○ Partial Nudity: Full or partial exposure of the human anatomy except when exposing genitalia.

○ Nudity: Any exposure of the human genitalia.

○ Sexual Acts (graphic or text): Pictures or text exposing anyone or anything involved in explicit sexual acts and lewd and lascivious behavior, including masturbation, copulation, pedophilia, intimacy and involving nude or partially nude people in heterosexual, bisexual, lesbian or homosexual encounters. Also includes phone sex ads, dating services, adult personals, CD-ROM and videos.

○ Gross Depictions (graphic or text): Pictures or descriptive text of anyone or anything which are crudely vulgar, deficient in civility or behavior, or showing scatological impropriety. Includes such depictions as maiming, bloody figures, indecent depiction of bodily functions.

○ Racism/Ethnic Impropriety: Prejudice or discrimination against any race or ethnic culture. Ethnic or racist jokes and slurs. Any text that elevates one race over another.

○ Satanic/Cult: Worship of the devil; affinity for evil, wickedness. Sects or groups that potentially coerce individuals to grow, and keep, membership.

○ Drugs/Drug Culture: Topics dealing with the use of illegal drugs for entertainment. This would exclude current illegal drugs used for medicinal purposes (e.g., drugs used to treat victims of AIDS). Includes substances used for other than their primary purpose to alter the individual's state of mind such as glue sniffing.

○ Militant/Extremist: Extremely aggressive and combative behaviors, radicalism, advocacy of extreme political measures.

Topics include extreme political groups that advocate violence as a means to achieve their goal.

○　Gambling: Of or relating to lotteries, casinos, betting, numbers games, on-line sports or financial betting including non-monetary dares.

○　Questionable/Illegal: Material or activities of a dubious nature which may be illegal in any or all jurisdictions, such as illegal business schemes, chain letters, software piracy, and copyright infringement.

○　Alcohol, Beer & Wine: Material pertaining to the sale or consumption of alcoholic beverages. Also includes sites and information relating to tobacco products.

58.　Microsystems employs people to search the Internet for sites containing material in these categories. Since new sites are constantly coming online, Microsystems updates the CyberNOT list on a weekly basis. Once installed on the home PC, the copy of Cyber Patrol receives automatic updates to the CyberNOT list over the Internet every seven days.

59.　In February of 1996, Microsystems signed a licensing arrangement with CompuServe, one of the leading commercial online services with over 4.3 million subscribers. CompuServe provides Cyber Patrol free of charge to its subscribers. Microsystems the same month signed a licensing arrangement with Prodigy, another leading commercial online service with over 1.4 million subscribers. Prodigy will provide Cyber Patrol free of charge of its subscribers.

60.　Cyber Patrol is also available directly from Microsystems for $49.95, which includes a six month subscription to the CyberNOT blocked sites list (updated automatically once every seven days). After six months, parents can receive six months of additional updates for $19.95, or twelve months for $29.95.
Cyber Patrol Home Edition, a limited version of Cyber Patrol, is available free of charge on the Internet. To obtain either version,

parents download a seven day demonstration version of the full Cyber Patrol product from the Microsystems Internet World Wide Web Server. At the end of the seven day trial period, users are offered the opportunity to purchase the complete version of Cyber Patrol or provide Microsystems some basic demographic information in exchange for unlimited use of the Home Edition. The demographic information is used for marketing and research purposes. Since January of 1996, over 10,000 demonstration copies of Cyber Patrol have been downloaded from Microsystems' Web site.

61. Cyber Patrol is also available from Retail outlets as NetBlocker Plus. NetBlocker Plus sells for $19.95, which includes five weeks of updates to the CyberNOT list.

62. Microsystems also sells Cyber Patrol into a growing market in schools. As more classrooms become connected to the Internet, many teachers want to ensure that their students can receive the benefit of the Internet without encountering material they deem educationally inappropriate.

63. Microsystems is working with the Recreational Software Advisory Council (RSAC), a non-profit corporation which developed rating systems for video games, to implement the RSAC rating system for the Internet.

64. The next release of Cyber Patrol, expected in second quarter of this year, will give parents the ability to use any PICS rating service, including the RSAC rating service, in addition to the Microsystems CyberNOT list.

65. In order to speed the implementation of PICS and encourage the development of PICS-compatible Internet applications, Microsystems maintains a server on the Internet which contains its CyberNOT list. The server provides software developers with access to a PICS rating service, and allows software developers to test their products' ability to interpret standard PICS labels. Microsystems is also offering its PICS client test program for

Windows free of charge. The client program can be used by developers of PICS rating services to test their services and products.

SurfWatch

66. Another software product, SurfWatch, is also designed to allow parents and other concerned users to filter unwanted material on the Internet. SurfWatch is available for both Apple Macintosh, Microsoft Windows, and Microsoft Windows 95 Operating Systems, and works with direct Internet Access Providers (e.g., Netcom, PSI, UUnet, AT&T, and more than 1000 other Internet Service Providers).

67. The suggested retail price of SurfWatch Software is $49.95, with a street price of between $20.00 and $25.00. The product is also available as part of CompuServe/Spry Inc.'s Internet in a Box for Kids, which includes access to Spry's Kids only Internet service and a copy of SurfWatch. Internet in a Box for Kids retails for approximately $30.00. The subscription service, which updates the SurfWatch blocked site list automatically with new sites each month, is available for $5.95 per month or $60.00 per year. The subscription is included as part of the Internet in a Box for Kids program, and is also provided as a low-cost option from Internet Service Providers.

68. SurfWatch is available at over 12,000 retail locations, including National stores such as Comp USA, Egghead Software, Computer City, and several national mail order outlets. SurfWatch can also be ordered directly from its own site on the World Wide Web, and through the Internet Shopping Network.

69. Plaintiffs America Online (AOL), Microsoft Network, and Prodigy all offer parental control options free of charge to their members. AOL has established an online area designed specifically for children. The "Kids Only" parental control feature allows

parents to establish an AOL account for their children that accesses only the Kids Only channel on America Online.(15)

70.   AOL plans to incorporate PICS-compatible capability into its standard Web browser software, and to make available to subscribers other PICS-compatible Web browsers, such as the Netscape software.

71.   Plaintiffs CompuServe and Prodigy give their subscribers the option of blocking all access to the Internet, or to particular media within their proprietary online content, such as bulletin boards and chat rooms.

72.   Although parental control software currently can screen for certain suggestive words or for known sexually explicit sites, it cannot now screen for sexually explicit images unaccompanied by suggestive text unless those who configure the software are aware of the particular site.

73.   Despite its limitations, currently available user-based software suggests that a reasonably effective method by which parents can prevent their children from accessing sexually explicit and other material which parents may believe is inappropriate for their children will soon be widely available.

Content on the Internet

74.   The types of content now on the Internet defy easy classification. The entire card catalogue of the Carnegie Library is on-line, together with journals, journal abstracts, popular magazines, and titles of compact discs. The director of the Carnegie Library, Robert Croneberger, testified that on-line services are the emerging trend in libraries generally. Plaintiff Hotwired Ventures LLC organizes its Web site into information regarding travel, news and commentary, arts and entertainment, politics, and types of drinks.

Plaintiff America Online, Inc., not only creates chat rooms for a broad variety of topics, but also allows members to create their own chat rooms to suit their own tastes. The ACLU uses an America Online chat room as an unmoderated forum for people to debate civil liberties issues. Plaintiffs' expert, Scott Bradner,(16) estimated that 15,000 newsgroups exist today, and he described his own interest in a newsgroup devoted solely to Formula 1 racing cars. America Online makes 15,000 bulletin boards available to its subscribers, who post between 200,000 and 250,000 messages each day. Another plaintiffs' expert, Harold Rheingold, participates in "virtual communities" that simulate social interaction. It is no exaggeration to conclude that the content on the Internet is as diverse as human thought.

75. The Internet is not exclusively, or even primarily, a means of commercial communication. Many commercial entities maintain Web sites to inform potential consumers about their goods and services, or to solicit purchases, but many other Web sites exist solely for the dissemination of non-commercial information. The other forms of Internet communication—e-mail, bulletin boards, newsgroups, and chat rooms—frequently have non-commercial goals. For the economic and technical reasons set forth in the following paragraphs, the Internet is an especially attractive means for not-for-profit entities or public interest groups to reach their desired audiences. There are examples in the parties' stipulation of some of the non-commercial uses that the Internet serves. Plaintiff Human Rights Watch, Inc., offers information on its Internet site regarding reported human rights abuses around the world. Plaintiff National Writers Union provides a forum for writers on issues of concern to them. Plaintiff Stop Prisoner Rape, Inc., posts text, graphics, and statistics regarding the incidence and prevention of rape in prisons. Plaintiff Critical Path AIDS Project, Inc., offers information on safer sex, the transmission of HIV, and the treatment of AIDS.

76.   Such diversity of content on the Internet is possible because the Internet provides an easy and inexpensive way for a speaker to reach a large audience, potentially of millions. The start-up and operating costs entailed by communication on the Internet are significantly lower than those associated with use of other forms of mass communication, such as television, radio, newspapers, and magazines. This enables operation of their own Web sites not only by large companies, such as Microsoft and Time Warner, but also by small, not-for-profit groups, such as Stop Prisoner Rape and Critical Path AIDS Project. The Government's expert, Dr. Dan R. Olsen,(17) agreed that creation of a Web site would cost between $1,000 and $15,000, with monthly operating costs depending on one's goals and the Web site's traffic. Commercial online services such as America Online allow subscribers to create Web pages free of charge. Any Internet user can communicate by posting a message to one of the thousands of newsgroups and bulletin boards or by engaging in an on-line "chat", and thereby reach an audience worldwide that shares an interest in a particular topic.

77.   The ease of communication through the Internet is facilitated by the use of hypertext markup language (HTML), which allows for the creation of "hyperlinks" or "links". HTML enables a user to jump from one source to other related sources by clicking on the link. A link might take the user from Web site to Web site, or to other files within a particular Web site. Similarly, by typing a request into a search engine, a user can retrieve many different sources of content related to the search that the creators of the engine have collected.

78.   Because of the technology underlying the Internet, the statutory term "content provider,"(18) which is equivalent to the traditional "speaker," may actually be a hybrid of speakers. Through the use of HTML, for example, Critical Path and Stop Prisoner Rape link their Web sites to several related databases, and a user can immediately jump from the home pages of these organizations to the

related databases simply by clicking on a link. America Online creates chat rooms for particular discussions but also allows subscribers to create their own chat rooms. Similarly, a newsgroup gathers postings on a particular topic and distributes them to the newsgroup's subscribers. Users of the Carnegie Library can read on-line versions of Vanity Fair and Playboy, and America Online's subscribers can peruse the New York Times, Boating, and other periodicals. Critical Path, Stop Prisoner Rape, America Online and the Carnegie Library all make available content of other speakers over whom they have little or no editorial control.

79. Because of the different forms of Internet communication, a user of the Internet may speak or listen interchangeably, blurring the distinction between "speakers" and "listeners" on the Internet. Chat rooms, e-mail, and newsgroups are interactive forms of communication, providing the user with the opportunity both to speak and to listen.

80. It follows that unlike traditional media, the barriers to entry as a speaker on the Internet do not differ significantly from the barriers to entry as a listener. Once one has entered cyberspace, one may engage in the dialogue that occurs there. In the argot of the medium, the receiver can and does become the content provider, and vice-versa.

81. The Internet is therefore a unique and wholly new medium of worldwide human communication.

Sexually Explicit Material On the Internet

82. The parties agree that sexually explicit material exists on the Internet. Such material includes text, pictures, and chat, and includes bulletin boards, newsgroups, and the other forms of Internet communication, and extends from the modestly titillating to the hardest-core.

83. There is no evidence that sexually-oriented material is the primary type of content on this new medium. Purveyors of such material take advantage of the same ease of access available to all users of the Internet, including establishment of a Web site.

84. Sexually explicit material is created, named, and posted in the same manner as material that is not sexually explicit. It is possible that a search engine can accidentally retrieve material of a sexual nature through an imprecise search, as demonstrated at the hearing. Imprecise searches may also retrieve irrelevant material that is not of a sexual nature. The accidental retrieval of sexually explicit material is one manifestation of the larger phenomenon of irrelevant search results.

85. Once a provider posts content on the Internet, it is available to all other Internet users worldwide. Similarly, once a user posts a message to a newsgroup or bulletin board, that message becomes available to all subscribers to that newsgroup or bulletin board. For example, when the UCR/California Museum of Photography posts to its Web site nudes by Edward Weston and Robert Mapplethorpe to announce that its new exhibit will travel to Baltimore and New York City, those images are available not only in Los Angeles, Baltimore, and New York City, but also in Cincinnati, Mobile, or Beijing—wherever Internet users live. Similarly, the safer sex instructions that Critical Path posts to its Web site, written in street language so that the teenage receiver can understand them, are available not just in Philadelphia, but also in Provo and Prague. A chat room organized by the ACLU to discuss the United States Supreme Court's decision in FCC v. Pacifica Foundation would transmit George Carlin's seven dirty words to anyone who enters. Messages posted to a newsgroup dedicated to the Oklahoma City bombing travel to all subscribers to that newsgroup.

86. Once a provider posts its content on the Internet, it cannot prevent that content from entering any community. Unlike the news-

paper, broadcast station, or cable system, Internet technology necessarily gives a speaker a potential worldwide audience. Because the Internet is a network of networks (as described above in Findings 1 through 4), any network connected to the Internet has the capacity to send and receive information to any other network. Hotwired Ventures, for example, cannot prevent its materials on mixology from entering communities that have no interest in that topic.

87. Demonstrations at the preliminary injunction hearings showed that it takes several steps to enter cyberspace. At the most fundamental level, a user must have access to a computer with the ability to reach the Internet (typically by way of a modem). A user must then direct the computer to connect with the access provider, enter a password, and enter the appropriate commands to find particular data. On the World Wide Web, a user must normally use a search engine or enter an appropriate address. Similarly, accessing newsgroups, bulletin boards, and chat rooms requires several steps.

88. Communications over the Internet do not "invade" an individual's home or appear on one's computer screen unbidden. Users seldom encounter content "by accident." A document's title or a description of the document will usually appear before the document itself takes the step needed to view it, and in many cases the user will receive detailed information about a site's content before he or she need take the step to access the document. Almost all sexually explicit images are preceded by warnings as to the content. Even the Government's witness, Agent Howard Schmidt, Director of the Air Force Office of Special Investigation, testified that the "odds are slim" that a user would come across a sexually explicit site by accident.

89. Evidence adduced at the hearing showed significant differences between Internet communications and communications received by radio or television. Although content on the Internet is just a

few clicks of a mouse away from the user, the receipt of information on the Internet requires a series of affirmative steps more deliberate and directed than merely turning a dial. A child requires some sophistication and some ability to read to retrieve material and thereby to use the Internet unattended.

Obstacles to Age Verification on the Internet

90. There is no effective way to determine the identity or the age of a user who is accessing material through e-mail, mail exploders, newsgroups or chat rooms. An e-mail address provides no authoritative information about the addressee, who may use an e-mail "alias" or an anonymous remailer. There is also no universal or reliable listing of e-mail addresses and corresponding names or telephone numbers, and any such listing would be or rapidly become incomplete. For these reasons, there is no reliable way in many instances for a sender to know if the e-mail recipient is an adult or a minor. The difficulty of e-mail age verification is compounded for mail exploders such as listservs, which automatically send information to all e-mail addresses on a sender's list. Government expert Dr. Olsen agreed that no current technology could give a speaker assurance that only adults were listed in a particular mail exploder's mailing list.

91. Because of similar technological difficulties, individuals posting a message to a newsgroup or engaging in chat room discussions cannot ensure that all readers are adults, and Dr. Olsen agreed. Although some newsgroups are moderated, the moderator's control is limited to what is posted and the moderator cannot control who receives the messages.

92. The Government offered no evidence that there is a reliable way to ensure that recipients and participants in such fora can be screened for age. The Government presented no evidence

demonstrating the feasibility of its suggestion that chat rooms, newsgroups and other fora that contain material deemed indecent could be effectively segregated to "adult" or "moderated" areas of cyberspace.

93. Even if it were technologically feasible to block minors' access to newsgroups and similar fora, there is no method by which the creators of newsgroups which contain discussions of art, politics or any other subject that could potentially elicit "indecent" contributions could limit the blocking of access by minors to such "indecent" material and still allow them access to the remaining content, even if the overwhelming majority of that content was not indecent.

94. Likewise, participants in MUDs (Multi-User Dungeons) and MUSEs (Multi-User Simulation Environments) do not know whether the other participants are adults or minors. Although MUDs and MUSEs require a password for permanent participants, they need not give their real name nor verify their age, and there is no current technology to enable the administrator of these fantasy worlds to know if the participant is an adult or a minor.

95. Unlike other forms of communication on the Internet, there is technology by which an operator of a World Wide Web server may interrogate a user of a Web site. An HTML document can include a fill-in-the-blank "form" to request information from a visitor to a Web site, and this information can be transmitted back to the Web server and be processed by a computer program, usually a Common Gateway Interface (cgi) script. The Web server could then grant or deny access to the information sought. The cgi script is the means by which a Web site can process a fill-in form and thereby screen visitors by requesting a credit card number or adult password.

96. Content providers who publish on the World Wide Web via one of the large commercial online services, such as America Online

or CompuServe, could not use an online age verification system that requires cgi script because the server software of these online services available to subscribers cannot process cgi scripts. There is no method currently available for Web page publishers who lack access to cgi scripts to screen recipients online for age.

The Practicalities of the Proffered Defenses

Note: The Government contends the CDA makes available three potential defenses to all content providers on the Internet: credit card verification, adult verification by password or adult identification number, and "tagging".

Credit Card Verification

97. Verification(19) of a credit card number over the Internet is not now technically possible. Witnesses testified that neither Visa nor Mastercard considers the Internet to be sufficiently secure under the current technology to process transactions in that manner. Although users can and do purchase products over the Internet by transmitting their credit card number, the seller must then process the transaction with Visa or Mastercard off-line using phone lines in the traditional way. There was testimony by several witnesses that Visa and Mastercard are in the process of developing means of credit card verification over the Internet.

98. Verification by credit card, if and when operational, will remain economically and practically unavailable for many of the non-commercial plaintiffs in these actions. The Government's expert "suspect[ed]" that verification agencies would decline to process a card unless it accompanied a commercial transaction. There was no evidence to the contrary.

99. There was evidence that the fee charged by verification agencies to process a card, whether for a purchase or not, will preclude use of the credit-card verification defense by many non-profit, non-commercial Web sites, and there was no evidence to the contrary. Plaintiffs' witness Patricia Nell Warren, an author whose free Web site allows users to purchase gay and lesbian literature, testified that she must pay $1 per verification to a verification agency. Her Web site can absorb this cost because it arises in connection with the sale of books available there.

100. Using credit card possession as a surrogate for age, and requiring use of a credit card to enter a site, would impose a significant economic cost on non-commercial entities. Critical Path, for example, received 3,300 hits daily from February 4 through March 4, 1996. If Critical Path must pay a fee every time a user initially enters its site, then, to provide free access to its non-commercial site, it would incur a monthly cost far beyond its modest resources. The ACLU's Barry Steinhardt testified that maintenance of a credit card verification system for all visitors to the ACLU's Web site would require it to shut down its Web site because the projected cost would exceed its budget.

101. Credit card verification would significantly delay the retrieval of information on the Internet. Dr. Olsen, the expert testifying for the Government, agreed that even "a minute is [an] absolutely unreasonable [delay] . . . [P]eople will not put up with a minute." Plaintiffs' expert Donna Hoffman similarly testified that excessive delay disrupts the "flow" on the Internet and stifles both "hedonistic" and "goal-directed" browsing.

102. Imposition of a credit card requirement would completely bar adults who do not have a credit card and lack the resources to obtain one from accessing any blocked material. At this time, credit card verification is effectively unavailable to a substantial number of Internet content providers as a potential defense to the CDA.

Adult Verification by Password

103. The Government offered very limited evidence regarding the operation of existing age verification systems, and the evidence offered was not based on personal knowledge. AdultCheck and Verify, existing systems which appear to be used for accessing commercial pornographic sites, charge users for their services. Dr. Olsen admitted that his knowledge of these services was derived primarily from reading the advertisements on their Web pages. He had not interviewed any employees of these entities, had not personally used these systems, had no idea how many people are registered with them, and could not testify to the reliability of their attempt at age verification.

104. At least some, if not almost all, non-commercial organizations, such as the ACLU, Stop Prisoner Rape or Critical Path AIDS Project, regard charging listeners to access their speech as contrary to their goals of making their materials available to a wide audience free of charge.

105. It would not be feasible for many non-commercial organizations to design their own adult access code screening systems because the administrative burden of creating and maintaining a screening system and the ongoing costs involved is beyond their reach. There was testimony that the costs would be prohibitive even for a commercial entity such as HotWired, the online version of Wired magazine.

106. There is evidence suggesting that adult users, particularly casual Web browsers, would be discouraged from retrieving information that required use of a credit card or password. Andrew Anker testified that HotWired has received many complaints from its members about HotWired's registration system, which requires only that a member supply a name, e-mail address and self-created password. There is concern by commercial content providers that age verification requirements would decrease

advertising and revenue because advertisers depend on a demonstration that the sites are widely available and frequently visited.

107. Even if credit card verification or adult password verification were implemented, the Government presented no testimony as to how such systems could ensure that the user of the password or credit card is in fact over 18. The burdens imposed by credit card verification and adult password verification systems make them effectively unavailable to a substantial number of Internet content providers.

The Government's "Tagging" Proposal

108. The feasibility and effectiveness of "tagging" to restrict children from accessing "indecent" speech, as proposed by the Government has not been established. "Tagging" would require content providers to label all of their "indecent" or "patently offensive" material by imbedding a string of characters, such as "XXX," in either the URL or HTML. If a user could install software on his or her computer to recognize the "XXX" tag, the user could screen out any content with that tag. Dr. Olsen proposed a "-L18" tag, an idea he developed for this hearing in response to Mr. Bradner's earlier testimony that certain tagging would not be feasible.

109. The parties appear to agree that it is technologically feasible— "trivial", in the words of plaintiffs' expert—to imbed tags in URLs and HTML, and the technology of tagging underlies both plaintiffs' PICS proposal and the Government's "-L18" proposal.

110. The Government's tagging proposal would require all content providers that post arguably "indecent" material to review all of their online content, a task that would be extremely burdensome for organizations that provide large amounts of material online which cannot afford to pay a large staff to review all of that material. The Carnegie Library would be required to hire numerous additional

employees to review its on-line files at an extremely high cost to its limited budget. The cost and effort would be substantial for the Library and frequently prohibitive for others. Witness Kiroshi Kuromiya testified that it would be impossible for his organization, Critical Path, to review all of its material because it has only one full and one part-time employee.

111. The task of screening and tagging cannot be done simply by using software which screens for certain words, as Dr. Olsen acknowledged, and we find that determinations as to what is indecent require human judgment.

112. In lieu of reviewing each file individually, a content provider could tag its entire site but this would prevent minors from accessing much material that is not "indecent" under the CDA.

113. To be effective, a scheme such as the -L18 proposal would require a worldwide consensus among speakers to use the same tag to label "indecent" material. There is currently no such consensus, and no Internet speaker currently labels its speech with the -L18 code or with any other widely-recognized label.

114. Tagging also assumes the existence of software that recognizes the tags and takes appropriate action when it notes tagged speech. Neither commercial Web browsers nor user-based screening software is currently configured to block a -L18 code. Until such software exists, all speech on the Internet will continue to travel to whomever requests it, without hindrance. Labeling speech has no effect in itself on the transmission (or not) of that speech. Neither plaintiffs nor the Government suggest that tagging alone would shield minors from speech or insulate a speaker from criminal liability under the CDA. It follows that all speech on any topic that is available to adults will also be available to children using the Internet (unless it is blocked by screening software running on the computer the child is using).

115. There is no way that a speaker can use current technology to know if a listener is using screening software.

116. Tags can not currently activate or deactivate themselves depending on the age or location of the receiver. Critical Path, which posts on-line safer sex instructions, would be unable to imbed tags that block its speech only in communities where it may be regarded as indecent. Critical Path, for example, must choose either to tag its site (blocking its speech in all communities) or not to tag, blocking its speech in none.

The Problems of Offshore Content and Caching

117. A large percentage, perhaps 40% or more, of content on the Internet originates outside the United States. At the hearing, a witness demonstrated how an Internet user could access a Web site of London (which presumably is on a server in England), and then link to other sites of interest in England. A user can sometimes discern from a URL that content is coming from overseas, since InterNIC allows a content provider to imbed a country code in a domain name.(20) Foreign content is otherwise indistinguishable from domestic content (as long as it is in English), since foreign speech is created, named, and posted in the same manner as domestic speech. There is no requirement that foreign speech contain a country code in its URL. It is undisputed that some foreign speech that travels over the Internet is sexually explicit.

118. The use of "caching" makes it difficult to determine whether the material originated from foreign or domestic sources. Because of the high cost of using the trans- Atlantic and trans-Pacific cables, and because the high demand on those cables leads to bottleneck delays, content is often "cached", or temporarily stored, on servers in the United States. Material from a foreign source in Europe can travel over the trans-Atlantic cable to the receiver in the United States, and pass through a domestic caching server which then stores a copy for subsequent retrieval. This domestic

caching server, rather than the original foreign server, will send the material from the cache to the subsequent receivers, without placing a demand on the trans-oceanic cables. This shortcut effectively eliminates most of the distance for both the request and the information and, hence, most of the delay. The caching server discards the stored information according to its configuration (e.g., after a certain time or as the demand for the information diminishes). Caching therefore advances core Internet values: the cheap and speedy retrieval of information.

119. Caching is not merely an international phenomenon. Domestic content providers store popular domestic material on their caching servers to avoid the delay of successive searches for the same material and to decrease the demand on their Internet connection. America Online can cache the home page of the New York Times on its servers when a subscriber first requests it, so that subsequent subscribers who make the same request will receive the same home page, but from America Online's caching service rather than from the New York Times's server.(21)

120. Put simply, to follow the example in the prior paragraph, America Online has no control over the content that the New York Times posts to its Web site, and the New York Times has no control over America Online's distribution of that content from a caching server.

Anonymity

121. Anonymity is important to Internet users who seek to access sensitive information, such as users of the Critical Path AIDS Project's Web site, the users, particularly gay youth, of Queer Resources Directory, and users of Stop Prisoner Rape (SPR). Many members of SPR's mailing list have asked to remain anonymous due to the stigma of prisoner rape.

Plaintiffs' Choices Under the CDA

122. Many speakers who display arguably indecent content on the Internet must choose between silence and the risk of prosecution. The CDA's defenses—credit card verification, adult access codes, and adult personal identification numbers —are effectively unavailable for non-commercial, not-for-profit entities.

123. The plaintiffs in this action are businesses, libraries, non-commercial and not-for-profit organizations, and educational societies and consortia. Although some of the material that plaintiffs post online—such as information regarding protection from AIDS, birth control or prison rape—is sexually explicit and may be considered "indecent" or "patently offensive" in some communities, none of the plaintiffs is a commercial purveyor of what is commonly termed "pornography."

Index